lonely ⊙ planet

POCKET

PRAGUE

TOP EXPERIENCES • LOCAL LIFE

T0021677

MARK BAKER, MARC DI DUCA

Contents

Plan Your Trip 4

Municipal House (p91) HEIDAR_NOURI/SHUTTERSTOCK ©

Explore Prague 33

Survival Guide 147

Special Features

Welcome to Prague

More than three decades after the Velvet Revolution drew back the curtain on this intoxicating maze of winding cobblestone alleyways, the 'city of a hundred spires' thrills visitors with dramatic Gothic and baroque architecture. It offers down-to-earth pubs, fin-de-siècle cafes, eclectic art collections and the regal Prague Castle – the world's largest – looming high over the capital city.

Prague's Top Experiences

Explore Prague Castle (p36)

Marvel at St Vitus Cathedral (p42)

Gather in the Old town Square (p84)

Walk Across Iconic Charles Bridge (p86)

Gain Insight at the Jewish Museum (p70)

Wander the Old Jewish Cemetery (p72)

Hike Up Petřín Hill (p54)

Admire the Baroque Beauty of Loreta (p44)

Stroll along Buzzing Wenceslas Square (p102)

Get Your Art Fix at Veletržní Palác (p138)

Dining Out

AHANOV MICHAEL/SHUTTERSTOCK ©

The restaurant scene in Prague gets better with each passing year. There has been an explosion in vegetarian and vegan restaurants, though meat is bigger than ever, both in traditional Czech restaurants and in fashionable burger joints.

Czech Cuisine

Czech food in Prague can be hit-and-miss. Traditional dishes such as roast pork and sliced bread dumplings (*vepřová pečeně s knedlíky*) or roast beef in cream sauce (*svíčková na smetaně*) can be bland or memorable (when prepared by someone who cares) so choose your restaurants carefully. Other Czech staples include pork knuckle (*vepřové koleno*), duck (*kachna*) and goulash (*guláš*; pictured), served with beef or pork and bread dumplings.

International Foods

International food trends come and go with the same regularity as in other large cities. Alongside standard international cuisines such as French and Italian, Czechs have developed a taste for good Indian and sushi as well as for Vietnamese and Mexican.

The latest trends include burgers as well as vegan and artisanal food.

Vegetarian Options

The last decade or so has witnessed a revolution in healthy dining, with a growing number of vegetarian and vegan restaurants sprouting up around town. Alas, vegetarian options at traditional Czech restaurants seem to be as limited, with the best bet being the ubiquitous (but often excellent) fried cheese (*smažený sýr*), served with a dollop of cranberry and/or tartar sauce.

TUPUNGATO/SHUTTERSTOCK ©

Best Fine Dining

Field Michelin-starred dining in the Old Town. (p77)

Augustine Relaxed sophistication combined with the restaurant's own beer. (p61)

Best Czech Cuisine

U Modré Kachničky Beautiful, classy restaurant in Malá Strana where the speciality is duck in many guises. (p62)

The Eatery Sophisticated Holešovice restaurant serving modern takes on Czech classics. (p142)

Vinohradský Parlament A 21st-century take on a Czech pub. (p133)

Best for Vegetarians

Vegan's Prague Completely plant-based restaurant on the main tourist route through Malá Strana. (p63)

Lehká Hlava Exotic dining room with an emphasis on fresh preparation. (p96)

Best for a Quick Lunch

Mistral Café Relaxing Old Town bistro, perfect for breakfast or lunch. (p79)

Havelská Koruna Self-service canteen serving cheap, institutional Czech food. (p96)

Hostinec U Tunelu Quality lunch menu at an atmospheric tavern. (p134)

Top Tips

• Some places charge a *couvert* (to cover the cost of bread); this should be marked on menus.

• Restaurants around Old Town Square are often sub-par and orientated toward tourists.

Bar Open

Drinking is a Czech national pastime, so it's no surprise that Prague is an imbiber's playground. On practically every corner, there's a pub, wine bar, beer hall or cocktail lounge. Despite an increase in interest in wine and cocktails over the years, Prague remains a beer city, with the national brands now joined by quality microbrews.

MATT MUNRO/LONELY PLANET ©

Beer Basics

When it comes to beer *(pivo)*, Czechs prefer light-coloured lagers *(světlé)* to darker beers *(tmavé)*, though most pubs serve both. Pilsner Urquell is considered the best Czech brand, though Gambrinus, Budvar and Prague's own Staropramen are popular. Czech beers are usually labelled either *dvanáctka* (12-degree) or *desítka* (10-degree), but this doesn't refer to alcohol content (most beers are 4.5% to 5%). The 12-degree beers tend to be heavier and stronger than the 10-degree beers.

Microbrews & 'Tank' Beer

The global craft-beer trend has reached Czechia and is most pronounced in Prague, which boasts around a dozen brewpubs where DIY brewers proffer their own concoctions, usually accompanied by good, traditional Czech cooking. To compete with the microbrews, the larger breweries have come up with several innovations, including offering unfiltered *(ne-filtrované)* beer and hauling beer directly to pubs in supersized tanks (called *tankové pivo)*. Obscure beers from around the Czechia are also well worth trying.

Best for Beer

Prague Beer Museum Not actually a museum but a hugely popular pub, with 30 varieties on tap. (p129)

Klášterní Pivovar Strahov Excellent microbrew beer at the Strahov Monastery. (p51)

U Zlatého Tygra The classic Prague drinking den, where Václav Havel took Bill Clinton in 1994 to show him a real Czech pub. (p96)

CUM OKOLO/ALAMY STOCK PHOTO ©

Pivovarský Dům Benedict Popular microbrewery with several beers on tap and decent Czech food. (p121)

Letná Beer Garden A big beer garden with stunning views over Prague. (pictured; p143)

U Tří Růží Tradition-reviving brewpub cooking up several different types of lager. (p96)

Best Cocktail Bars

Hemingway Bar Snug and sophisticated hideaway. (p97)

Tretter's New York Bar Upmarket New York-style cocktail bar. (p80)

Best for Wine

Le Caveau Cosy Vinohrady watering hole and deli featuring excellent French wine. (p129)

Café Kaaba Retro cafe that stocks wines from around the world. (p135)

Best Cafes

Grand Cafe Orient A stunning cubist gem with a sunny balcony. (p97)

Cafe Louvre An agreeable grand cafe and billiards hall. (p120)

Kavárna Obecní Dům Legendary Viennese-style coffee house inside an art-nouveau landmark. (p97)

Café Savoy Gorgeous coffee house that does a lavish breakfast and good lunches. (p61)

Kavárna Slavia Famous cafe opposite the National Theatre. (p120)

Top Tips

○ Pub tabs, particularly in traditional places, are often recorded on a slip of paper on your table; don't write on it or lose it.

○ To pay up and go, say *zaplatím* (I'll pay).

Treasure Hunt

DENDENAL/SHUTTERSTOCK ©

Prague doesn't initially seem to be a particularly inspiring shopping city. But if you know where to look, you can find great, classic souvenirs: Bohemian crystal and glassware, garnets and puppets. Farm-produced beauty products and old-school children's toys also make great gifts.

For mainstream shopping, central Na Příkopě boasts international chains from H&M to Zara. For the most part, you can put your wallet away along Wenceslas Square. Instead, explore the Old Town's winding alleyways. Ritzy Pařížská is lined with luxury brands. Dlouhá, Dušní and surrounding streets house some original fashion boutiques, while even central Celetná contains a worthwhile stop or two.

Best for Unique Souvenirs

Orel & Friends Stocks authentic, top-notch souvenirs made across Czechia. (p64)

Manufaktura Specialises in traditional Czech crafts and wooden toys. (pictured; p99)

Bric A Brac Aladdin's cave of yesteryear jumble. (p99)

Botanicus Natural cosmetics and local, hand-crafted items. (p99)

Best for Design & Glass

Modernista Czech cubist and art-deco design with cool ceramics, jewellery, posters and books. (p99)

Moser Ornate Bohemian glass objects. (p113)

Artěl Traditional glass-making meets modern design in this stylish shop in Malá Strana. (p65)

Best for Books & Toys

Shakespeare & Sons More than just a bookshop – a congenial literary hangout. (p65)

Kavka Coffee-table art books you won't find anywhere else. (p99)

Under the Radar Prague

DAVID KRASENSKY/SHUTTERSTOCK ©

Prague's central core is so lively that many visitors might be mistaken for thinking this is all the city has to offer. The fact is, Prague stretches out in all directions and to places that visitors rarely, if ever, see. Come out to the neighbourhoods to find out what really makes Prague tick.

Cool Karlín

It's difficult to tell where the dice will fall in coming years as far as Prague's coolest up-and-coming neighbourhood is concerned. But there's a good chance it will still be Karlín, the hottest area that most tourists never visit.

Stunning Stromovka

Prague's biggest central park, Stromovka, has gotten a huge makeover in the past few years. City planners have added new ponds and flowerbeds, dressed up the meadows and revamped old buildings, like the grand old Šlechta's Restaurant (Šlechtova restaurace).

Experiences

The number of people and companies offering experiences – guided historical tours, wine- or beer-drinking outings, absinthe nights, boating and biking trips – has exploded. These outings are invariably fun and add new dimensions to discovering the city.

Street Festivals

Every weekend from March through September seems to bring out another street festival somewhere around town. The theme can be almost anything: craft beers, burgers, food trucks, farmers' markets. Praguers love them. Whatever the reason, you can bet it will be crowded.

Art & Museums

Prague has tonnes of museums scattered around the city. Most cater to specific interests, but alas, some of the collections are still of the old-school: static objects displayed behind thick glass. For art-lovers, the National Gallery's collections are particularly strong in medieval art, baroque and early-20th-century art.

ALBERTO ZAMORANO/SHUTTERSTOCK ©

Best Museums for Art

Veletržní Palác National Gallery's jaw-dropping collection of art from the 20th and 21st centuries. (p138)

Šternberg Palace National Gallery's collection of European art includes works by Goya and Rembrandt. (p49)

Mucha Museum Sensuous art-nouveau posters, paintings and decorative panels by Alfons Mucha. (p107)

Best Public Art

K Kafka's rotating head is now Prague's most prominent piece of public art; by David Černý. (p118)

Miminka Creepy babies crawling atop the Žižkov TV Tower; by David Černý. (p133)

Proudy David Černý's sculpture features two guys relieving themselves into a puddle shaped like Czechia. (p57)

Best General Museums

Jewish Museum Displays the development of centuries of Jewish life. (pictured; p70)

National Technical Museum Czechia's industrial heritage on riotous display. (p141)

National Museum Better for the interiors than for the permanent exhibition. (p107)

Retro Muzeum Praha Mash-up of communist-era kitsch and contemporary history. (p92)

Top Tips

○ Most museums offer discounted family tickets.

○ The **Prague CoolPass** (www.praguecoolpass.com) offers free or discounted entry to around 70 sights.

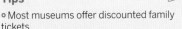

LGBTIQ+ Travellers

Prague is a non-judgmental destination for LGBTIQ+ travellers. Homosexuality is legal, and since 2006 gay couples have been able to form registered partnerships. The city has a lively gay scene, anchored mainly in Vinohrady, and is home to Central Europe's biggest annual gay pride march, held in August.

ALZBETA IVANCENKOVA/SHUTTERSTOCK ©

Resources

Two good online sources of information are **Travel Gay Europe** (www.travel-gay.com) and **Prague Gay Travel Guide** (www.patroc.com/gay/prague). Both maintain up-to-date lists of the best bars and clubs. **Prague City Tourism** (www.prague.eu) maintains a list of LGBTIQ+ friendly hotels and pensions.

Best Cafes & Bars

Saints (www.facebook.com/thesaintsbar) Laid-back, friendly basement bar with good drinks.

Café Celebrity (www.celebritycafe.cz) Vinohrady standby that's great for coffee and people-watching.

Q Cafe (www.q-cafe.cz) Low-key drinks bar that attracts a youthful clientele.

Best Clubs & Dance

Termix (www.club-termix.cz) Industrial techno vibe (lots of shiny steel, glass and plush sofas) and a young crowd that includes as many tourists as locals. (p135)

Friends Club (www.friendsclub.cz) Good spot to sit back with a drink and check out the crowd, or join in the party spirit on assorted theme nights.

Club Termax (www.facebook.com/clubmax.cz) Enormous dance club in the heart of Vinohrady.

Best Events

Mezipatra (www.mezipatra.cz) Annual gay and lesbian film festival held in November.

QueerBall (www.queerball.cz) Yearly fancy-dress ball normally held in September in Vinohrady.

Prague Pride (www.praguepride.cz) Annual gay pride march every August.

For Kids

Czechs are very family-oriented, so there are plenty of activities for children around the city. An increasing number of Prague restaurants cater specifically for children, with play areas and so on, and many offer a children's menu – even if they don't, they can usually provide smaller portions for a lower price.

PRITYKIN_NIKITA/SHUTTERSTOCK ©

Into the Fresh Air

A great outing for kids (and parents) is Prague Zoo, located north of the centre in Troja. In addition, there are several other patches of green around town, such as Stromovka, where you can spread a blanket and let the kids run free.

Petřín is a beautiful park on a hill where parents and kids alike can take a break from sightseeing, and climb the Petřín Lookout Tower for terrific views over Prague.

Best Outdoor Activities

Stromovka Prague's largest central park, with lots of playgrounds. (p145)

Prague Zoo Aside from the animals, attractions include a miniature cable car. (pictured; p142)

Petřín Funicular Kids will get a thrill riding this funicular to the top of the hill. (p55)

Best Indoor Activities

National Technical Museum A must-stop for inquisitive adolescents and tech-savvy parents. (p141)

Museum of the Senses The interactive exhibits bamboozle young visitors with optical illusions. (p118)

Miniature Museum Weird but fascinating place that will boggle kids' (and adults') minds. (p49)

Top Tips

○ Kids up to age 15 normally pay half-price for attractions (kids under six are free).

○ On public transport, kids 15 years and under ride for free (always carry a valid picture ID).

For Free

Once famously inexpensive, Prague is no longer cheap – there's little on offer without a price attached. That said, in a city this beautiful, you don't need to spend lots of time (or money) on pricey museums. The parks and gardens, including the hilltop vista from Letná Gardens, are free, as is the street entertainment on Charles Bridge.

JAROSLAW GRUDZINSKI/SHUTTERSTOCK ©

Prague Castle Without a Ticket

Admission to the interiors of Prague Castle, including St Vitus Cathedral, costs a bit. But many people don't realise that the castle grounds, including the surrounding gardens, are free to roam at your leisure. The highlights of a visit are the views over Malá Strana and the hourly changing of the guard (pictured); the grandest show is performed daily at noon.

Best Free Sights

Charles Bridge Prague's best single experience, crossing Charles Bridge, is completely free. (p86)

Nový Svět Quarter A delightful alternative to Prague Castle's Golden Lane. (p50)

Petřín Hill Entrance to the park is gratis; skip the funicular and just hike up. (p54)

Astronomical Clock The hourly chiming is public and free. (p85)

Vyšehrad Cemetery This beautiful cemetery is the final resting place for composers Smetana and Dvořák, as well as art-nouveau artist Alfons Mucha. (p125)

Letná Gardens The sweeping views are free; drinks from the beer garden cost extra. (p141)

Top Tips

⊙ Ask at tourist information offices about free concerts, theatrical performances and cultural events happening during your visit.

⊙ Visits to most churches (except St Vitus Cathedral and St Nicholas Church) are free.

Architecture

MICHAL SANCA/SHUTTERSTOCK ©

Prague is an open-air museum of architecture; most of the centre enjoys Unesco protection. Its architectural heritage was built up over centuries, with the earliest Romanesque buildings dating back nearly 1000 years. Later, Renaissance, baroque, neoclassical and art-nouveau styles were added as fashions changed.

Best Romanesque & Gothic

Rotunda of St Martin This tiny circular church in Vyšehrad is reputedly Prague's oldest standing building and a surviving example of Romanesque architecture. (pictured; p125)

St Vitus Cathedral Gothic to the tips of its spires. (p42)

Charles Bridge Prague's most famous bridge is a Gothic landmark. (p86)

Best Renaissance & Baroque

St Nicholas Church In Malá Strana, this is the mother of all baroque churches. (p59)

Loreta This pilgrimage site is modelled after the Italian original. (p44)

Best National Revival & Art Nouveau

Municipal House Glittering art nouveau. (p91)

Grand Hotel Evropa Fading grandeur at this ornate art-nouveau hotel and cafe. (p103)

Best Modern Architecture

Church of the Most Sacred Heart of Our Lord Prague's most unusual church; by a Slovene architect. (p132)

Veletržní Palác Mammoth functionalist structure. (p138)

Top Tips

○ For more on architecture, take a tour with Prague Unknown (www.prahaneznama.cz).

○ *Prague: An Architectural Guide* is a photographic encyclopedia by Smith, Schonberg and Sedlakova.

History

Prague history reads like a novel, chock-full of characters riding the city's fortunes from the heights of the Holy Roman Empire to the depths of the Eastern bloc (with chills and spills in between). Fortunately, the city was spared mass destruction in WWII, and every building, from the castle to the corner shop, has a story.

SCULPTURES BY DAVID ČERNY
TOBIK/SHUTTERSTOCK ©

Best Royal Sights

Vyšehrad Citadel Where it all began – Prague's oldest fortification. (p125)

Prague Castle Seat of Czech power for 1000 years. (p36)

Astronomical Clock Ancient mechanical marvel that still chimes on the hour. (p85)

St Nicholas Church The height of Habsburg-inspired baroque splendour. (p59)

Best National Revival

National Museum Massive building at the top of Wenceslas Square that celebrates Czech national culture. (p107)

Municipal House Artnouveau apogee of art and national aspiration. (p91)

National Theatre Built to showcase emerging Czech music and drama. (p121)

Rudolfinum Impressive concert hall completed in 1884; served as the seat of the Czechoslovak Parliament between WWI and WWII. (p76)

Best for Modern History

National Memorial to the Heroes of the Heydrich Terror Site where seven Czechoslovak partisans took refuge from the Nazis – and met tragic ends – in 1942. (p119)

TV Tower Communist power at its most potent. (pictured; p132)

John Lennon Wall This graffiti-splattered memorial was repainted each time the secret police whitewashed over it. (p57)

Velvet Revolution Memorial Marks the spot where the Velvet Revolution kicked off on 17 November 1989. (p105)

National Monument The gruesome laboratory in the basement here was once used to try to preserve communist leader Klement Gottwald's decomposing body. It didn't work. (p131)

Responsible Travel

Follow these tips when you're in Prague to leave a lighter footprint, support local and have a positive impact on local communities.

DUCHY/SHUTTERSTOCK ©

Support Local

Look for authentic or locally made souvenirs, such as handcrafted items, crystal, jewellery or Czech-made toys, over mass-produced Russian nesting dolls and KGB fur hats that have nothing to do with Prague.

Skip phony 'trdelnik' (chimney cake) stands and opt instead for authentic Czech street food, such as the *koláče* (soft round pastries) at Kolatcherie. *Trdelnik* vendors sport signs saying how 'traditional' their products are; in truth, they're just gimmicks.

Fight Overtourism

Book accommodation directly with hotels, guesthouses and hosts rather than through short-term rental sites. These short-term rentals have led to sky-rocketing apartment prices for ordinary citizens and transformed blocks of the Old Town into heavily touristed areas.

Once you've seen the centre, visit some outlying districts – Prague's historical core is breathtaking, but you'll find more-authentic city life in residential neighbourhoods like Vinohrady and Holešovice.

Skip the big, mass-market pub crawls and opt instead to visit pubs in smaller parties of two or four people. These big crawls, sometimes involving dozens of people at a time, destroy the traditional pub atmosphere and clog the tiny streets with drunken revellers.

Leave a Small Footprint

Use public transport – ride-sharing apps are widely available but the cars clog up the roads and contribute to the city's dirty air. Metros and trams are fast and cheap.

Cycle Rekola (www.rekola. cz) bike shares (look for the pink bikes) are fun and an easy way to cover ground quickly. Avoid the electric scooters that litter the streets. Not only are they dangerous for inexperienced riders, but residents see them as nuisances.

When riding bikes (or scooters), stay off pavements and stick to roads

MARADON 333/SHUTTERSTOCK ©

and marked cycling paths. There's a great cycling path south along the Vltava River from the Naplavka (pictured right).

Resources

Bez Obalu (www.bezobalu. org) operates packaging-free stores throughout Prague and educates the general public on reducing packaging.

Pragulic (www.pragulic.cz) operates alternative walking tours, led by homeless people, to challenge stereotypes associated with homelessness and see the city from their perspective

Prague City Tourism (www. praguecitytourism.cz) is the tourism-promotion group dedicated to supporting a sustainable tourism economy. Check the website for various reports on the problems with tourism, such as overtourism, and measures the city is taking to address them.

Climate Change & Travel

It's impossible to ignore the impact we have when traveling and the importance of making changes where we can. Lonely Planet urges all travellers to engage with their travel carbon footprint. There are many carbon calculators online that allow travellers to estimate the carbon emissions generated by their journey; try resurgence.org/resources/carbon-calculator.html. Many airlines and booking sites offer travellers the option of offsetting the impact of greenhouse gas emissions by contributing to climate-friendly initiatives around the world. We continue to offset the carbon footprint of all Lonely Planet staff travel, while recognising this is a mitigation more than a solution.

Four Perfect Days

Day 1

Just one day in Prague? Focus on major sights. Start early, joining the crowd below the **Astronomical Clock** (p85) for the hourly chiming, then wander through the **Old Town Square** (p84), taking in the spectacular array of architectural styles and the spires of the **Church of Our Lady Before Týn** (p85). From there, amble through the winding alleys of the Old Town on your way to one of Prague's most famous landmarks, **Charles Bridge** (pictured; p86). Stop for lunch at **Cukrkávalimonáda** (p62) before hiking up to **Prague Castle** (p36) through Malá Strana. Visiting the castle and **St Vitus Cathedral** (p42) will take the rest of the day. For dinner, treat yourself to a traditional meal at **U Modré Kachničky** (p62) nearby.

Day 2

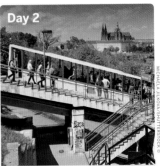

Spend the morning exploring the quaint backstreets and Kampa gardens of Malá Strana, one of the city's oldest districts. Catch the **Petřín Funicular** (pictured; p55) to enjoy sweeping views from the **Lookout Tower** (p55) at the top of Petřín Hill. From here, find the serene path that crosses over to the **Strahov Monastery** (p47), and then head downhill along Nerudova. Return to Kampa and treat yourself to a late lunch at **Café Savoy** (p61).

Cross the river in the afternoon to check out the **Jewish Museum** (p70). Later, stop by the box office of the **National Theatre** (p121) to see if any last-minute tickets are available for the opera or ballet. Before the show, have a light meal at **Cafe Louvre** (p120).

Day 3

Start with coffee at the famous **Kavárna Slavia** (p120), choosing a table looking across the river to Prague Castle. From here, walk up Národní třída to **Wenceslas Square** (pictured; p102), taking time to see the nearby sights, including the **National Museum** (p107) and the **St Wenceslas Statue** (p103). Plan lunch at **Výtopna** (p110).

From here it's an easy metro trip to **Vyšehrad** (p124), where you can wander the ruins and visit the graves of Dvořak and Mucha in the cemetery and admire the river views.

Spend the evening in Vinohrady or Žižkov, choosing one of the area's excellent restaurants, such as **Vinohradský Parlament** (p133) or **The Tavern** (p134).

Day 4

It's time to see a different part of Prague. Start on Old Town Square and walk down elegant Pařížská, before crossing the river and climbing to **Letná Gardens** (p141). Admire the views from the top, then make your way over to **Mr Hot Dog** (p143) or **Bistro 8** (p142) for an early lunch.

Suitably fortified, it's a short walk to the **National Technical Museum** (pictured; p141) – perfect if you've got kids. If you've still got the energy, visit Prague's best (and most underrated) art museum, **Veletržní Palác** (p138) before taking the tram back towards town. Enjoy a meal on the rooftop terrace at **U Prince** (p95) to lift a glass to this lovely city on your last night.

Need to Know

For detailed information, see Survival Guide (p147)

Currency
Czech crown (Koruna
česká; Kč)

Language
Czech

Visas
Generally not required
for stays of up to three
months.

Money
ATMs are widely
available and credit
cards are accepted at
nearly all restaurants
and hotels.

Mobile Phones
Czechia uses GSM 900,
compatible with mobile
phones from the rest of
Europe, Australia and
New Zealand (but not
most North American
phones).

Time
Central European Time
(GMT plus one hour).

Tipping
Standard practice
in pubs, cafes and
restaurants is to tip
10%.

Daily Budget

Budget: Less than €80
Dorm beds: €12–20
Cheap supermarkets for self-catering
Admission to major tourist attractions: €10

Midrange: €80–200
Double room: €120–200
Three-course dinner in casual restaurant: €30

Top end: More than €200
Double room or suite at luxury hotel: €200–260
Seven-course tasting menu in top restaurant: €120

Useful Websites

Lonely Planet (www.lonelyplanet.com/czech-republic/
prague) Destination info, hotel bookings, traveller forum
and more.

Prague City Tourism (www.prague.eu) Prague's official
tourism portal.

Expats.cz (www.expats.cz) English-language news and
current events website.

Prague Public Transit (www.dpp.cz) Handy journey plan-
ner for all public transport.

Arriving in Prague

Public transport and taxis are easily available from both arrival hubs.

✈ **Václav Havel Airport Prague**
Around 17km by road from the Old Town Square.

Airport Express (AE) bus runs every 30 minutes to Praha Hlavní Nádraží train station (100Kč).

Taxis wait outside the terminals and cost around 700Kč to the centre.

Bus 119 runs regularly to Nádraží Veleslavín metro station (40Kč).

🚆 **Praha Hlavní Nádraží Train Station**

The main train station is situated in Nové Město, near central Wenceslas Square.

Metro The station is on red line C, with direct connections to Holešovice and Vyšehrad. Change at either Můstek or Florenc for other destinations.

Walk The city centre is within walking distance.

Getting Around

Prague's public-transport system is one of Europe's best. Most visitors will get everywhere they need to on foot, metro or tram.

Ⓜ **Metro**
Prague's metro system runs from 5am to midnight, with fast, frequent service.

🚊 **Tram**
Travelling on trams is a quintessential Prague experience. Regular trams run from 5am to midnight. After midnight, night trams rumble across the city about every 40 minutes.

🚕 **Taxi**
Taxis are convenient, but it's safest to order a cab by phone. International ride-share services like Uber and Bolt operate in the city.

Prague Neighbourhoods

Prague Castle & Hradčany (p35)
This refined hilltop district is defined by the castle complex that gives Prague its dreamy, fairy-tale-like appearance.

Old Town Square & Staré Město (p83)
Gothic spires, art-nouveau architecture, a quirky astronomical clock and horse-drawn carriages crowd this colourful, famous old square.

Old Jewish Cemetery

Jewish Museum

Prague Castle
St Vitus Cathedral ◉ ◉

Loreta ◉

Charles Bridge ◉

Old Town Square & Astronomical Clock ◉

Petřín Hill ◉

Malá Strana & Petřín Hill (p53)
Quaint, cobblestoned streets, red roofs, ancient cloisters and a peaceful hillside park characterise Prague's charming 'Lesser Quarter'.

Nové Město (p115)
Cool modern architecture and quiet riverside cafes are the crowning glories of this underrated neighbourhood.

Holešovice (p137)
Beer gardens, contemporary art and huge parks characterise this laid-back district that's well off the tourist path.

Veletržní Palác 👁

Jewish Museum & Josefov (p69)
Today, Prague's one-time Jewish ghetto is home to a cluster of historic synagogues and the eerie Old Jewish Cemetery.

👁 *Wenceslas Square*

Wenceslas Square & Around (p101)
Once a horse market, this huge square has been the site of many important moments in Czech history.

Vinohrady & Žižkov (p127)
The locals' residential neighbourhood of choice, this leafy area contains many of Prague's hippest bars and cafes.

Explore
Prague

Prague's Walking Tours

Municipal House (p91) PYTY/SHUTTERSTOCK ©

Explore

Prague Castle & Hradčany

St Vitus Cathedral, rising from the heart of Prague Castle, is rarely out of view when you're wandering around Prague. The promontory on which the castle sits is called Hradčany, an area packed with fascinating sites, both religious and secular.

The Short List

○ **Prague Castle (p36)** *Seek out the exhibition in the vaults beneath the Old Royal Palace that documents the history of Czechia's most famous historical complex.*

○ **St Vitus Cathedral (p42)** *The Czechs' top temple is built in a hotchpotch of architectural styles and packed with artistic treasures.*

○ **Loreta (p44)** *One of the most significant places of pilgrimage, with the Santa Casa at its heart.*

○ **Strahov Library (p47)** *The country's largest and most ornate monastery library.*

○ **Golden Lane (p38)** *Street of miniature cottages at Prague castle, where Franz Kafka once stayed.*

Getting There & Around

🚃 Take 22 to Pražský hrad then walk five minutes, or to Pohořelec and then walk downhill.

Ⓜ Take Line A to Malostranská, then climb the steps.

Neighbourhood Map on p46

St Vitus Cathedral (p42) MIKHAIL MARKOVSKIY/SHUTTERSTOCK ©

Top Experience 📷
Explore Prague Castle

Known simply as hrad (castle) to locals, Prague Castle was founded by 9th-century Přemyslid princes and grew haphazardly as subsequent rulers extended out across the promontory. Today, it's a humungous complex with three large courtyards. Many Czech rulers have resided here; one notable exception is the first post-communist president, Václav Havel: in 1989, he plumped for the comforts of his own home instead.

◉ **MAP P46, E2**

Pražský hrad

www.hrad.cz

Hradčanské náměstí 1

adult/concession from 250/125Kč

🚊 22, 23,
Ⓜ Malostranská,

Castle Entrance

The castle's main gate, on Hradčany Square (Hradčanské náměstí), is flanked by huge, 18th-century statues of battling Titans that dwarf the castle guards below. Playwright-turned-president Václav Havel hired the Czech costume designer on the film *Amadeus* to redesign the guards' uniforms and instigated a changing-of-the-guard ceremony – the most impressive display is at noon.

Prague Castle Picture Gallery

In 1648 an invading Swedish army looted Emperor Rudolf II's art collection (as well as the original bronze statues in the Wallenstein Garden). The **gallery** in these converted Renaissance stables displays what was left, as well as replacement works, including some by Rubens, Tintoretto and Titian.

Plečnik Monolith

In the third courtyard, a noteworthy feature near St Vitus Cathedral is a huge granite monolith dedicated to the victims of WWI, designed by Slovene architect Jože Plečnik in 1928. Nearby is a copy of the castle's famous statue of St George slaying the dragon.

Old Royal Palace

The palace's highlight is the high-Gothic vaulted roof of **Vladislav Hall** (Vladislavský sál; 1493–1502), beneath which all the presidents of Czechia have been sworn in. There's also a balcony off the hall with great city views and a door to the former Bohemian Chancellery, where the Second Defenestration of Prague occurred in 1618.

★ **Top Tips**

o The castle buildings open at 9am; be there a few minutes early to beat the crowds.

o You'll need at least half a day to explore the castle grounds.

o Guided tours of the castle in English can be arranged in advance by calling 224 372 187. Tours last around an hour and leave from the information centres.

o To catch music and cultural events at the castle grounds, check out **Kultura na Hradě** (www.kulturanahrade.cz) for a schedule of events.

✗ **Take a Break**

There are a number of places scattered around the castle grounds to stop for a coffee or cold drink. A favourite – also good for lunch – is the lovely Lobkowicz Palace Café (p50), located on the ground level of Lobkowicz Palace.

Story of Prague Castle

One of the castle's most compelling **exhibitions** (www.hrad.cz), with an outstanding collection of armour, jewellery, glassware, furniture and other artefacts from more than 1000 years of the castle's history. A particularly memorable sight is the skeleton of the pre-Christian 'warrior', still encased in the earth where archaeologists found him within the castle grounds.

Basilica of St George

Behind a brick-red facade lies the Czechs' best-preserved Romanesque **church** (www.hrad.cz). The original was established in the 10th century by Vratislav I (the father of St Wenceslas), who is still buried here, as is St Ludmilla. It's also popular for small concert performances.

Golden Lane

The tiny, colourful cottages along this cobbled **alley** were built in the 16th century for the castle guard's sharpshooters, but were later used by goldsmiths, squatters and artists, including writer Franz Kafka, who stayed at his sister's house at No 22 from 1916 to 1917.

Basilica of St George

Kings & Castles

Prague's history, filled with royal betrayals, people being tossed out of windows, and one man famously being burnt at the stake, makes the Tudors look tame by comparison.

In the Beginning

The name 'Bohemia', still used to describe Czechia's western half, comes from a Celtic tribe, the Boii, who lived here for centuries before Slavic tribes arrived, around the 6th century. The Přemysl dynasty built the earliest section of today's Prague Castle in the 9th century, and also included one Václav, or Wenceslas, of 'Good King' Christmas-carol fame.

The Good Times

After the Přemyslid dynasty died out, Prague came under the control of the family that eventually produced Holy Roman Emperor Charles IV (1316–78). Under his rule, the city blossomed. Charles, whose mother was Czech, elevated Prague's official status and went on a construction spree, building the New Town (Nové Město) and Charles Bridge, founding Charles University and adding St Vitus Cathedral to the castle.

University rector Jan Hus led the 15th-century Hussite movement, which challenged what many saw as the corrupt practices of the Catholic Church. Hus was burned at the stake in Constance, Germany in 1415 for 'heresy' – this kicked off decades of sectarian fighting.

Habsburg Rule

In 1526 the Czech lands came under the rule of the Austrian Habsburgs. With the Reformation in full swing in Europe, tensions between the Catholic Habsburgs and reformist Czechs inevitably surfaced. In 1618 Bohemian rebels threw two Catholic councillors from a Prague Castle window, sparking the Thirty Years' War (1618–48). Following the defeat of the Czech nobility in 1620 at the Battle of White Mountain (Bílá Hora), the Czechs lost their independence to Austria for 300 years.

Rosenberg Palace

Originally built as the grand residence of the Rosenberg family, this 16th-century Renaissance-style **palace** was later repurposed by Empress Maria Theresa as a 'Residence for Noblewomen' to house 30 unmarried women at a time. Today, one section of the palace re-creates the style of an 18th-century noblewoman's apartment using artefacts from Prague Castle's depository.

Lobkowicz Palace

The 16th-century **Lobkowicz Palace** (www.lobkowicz.com) houses a private museum known as the Princely Collections, with priceless paintings, furniture and musical memorabilia. An included audio guide dictated by owner William Lobkowicz and his family brings the displays to life, making this one of the castle's most interesting attractions.

Royal Garden

Powder Bridge (Prašný most; 1540) spans the Stag Moat (Jelení příkop) en route to the spacious Renaissance-style **Royal Garden**, dating from 1534. The most beautiful building is the **Ball-Game House** (Míčovna; 1569), a masterpiece of Renaissance sgraffito, where the Habsburgs once played badminton. East is the **Summer Palace** (Letohrádek; 1538–60) and west the former **Riding School** (Jízdárna; 1695).

Southern Gardens

The three gardens lined up below the castle's southern wall – **Paradise Garden**, the **Hartig Garden** and the **Garden on the Ramparts** – offer superb views over Malá Strana's rooftops. Enter from the west via the New Castle Steps or from the east via the Old Castle Steps.

Visiting Prague Castle

Prague Castle recently changed it tour routes and prices. Now there is just one tour, which includes the Old Royal Palace, the Basilica of St George, Golden Lane and the cathedral. An extra ticket is required for the cathedral tower and for the Story of Prague Castle exhibition. Tickets are valid for two days but you can only visit each site once. Once you have bought your ticket you cannot get a refund. If you want to take snaps it will cost you 50Kč extra. Purchase all tickets etc at the ticket offices in the second and third courtyards. Your Prague Castle ticket is also valid for the Charles Bridge Museum (p87).

Prague Castle

Old
Castle Steps

Lobkowicz Palace
Café

Lobkowicz
Palace

Rosenberg
Palace

Golden
Lane

Stag Moat

Royal
Garden

Basilica of
St George

St George's
Square

Story of
Prague
Castle

Old
Royal
Palace

Southern
Gardens

Third
Courtyard

St Vitus
Cathedral

Plečnik
Monolith

Powder
Bridge

Information
Centre

Second
Courtyard

New
Castle
Steps

Prague Castle
Picture Gallery

Information
Centre

First
Courtyard

Castle
Entrance

Hradčany Sq

Top Experience 📸
Marvel at the grandeur of St Vitus Cathedral

Czechia's most important church was begun in 1344, and although it appears Gothic at first, much of St Vitus Cathedral was only completed in time for its belated consecration in 1929. The coronations of Bohemia's kings were held here until the mid-19th century. Today it's the seat of Prague's Archbishop and the final resting place of some of the nation's most illustrious figures.

◉ MAP P46, E2

Katedrála sv Víta

www.katedralasvate
hovita.cz

🚋 22, 23

Stained-Glass Windows

The interior is flooded with colour from stained-glass windows created by eminent Czech artists of the early 20th century. In the third chapel on the northern side is one by art-nouveau artist Alfons Mucha (pictured), depicting the lives of Sts Cyril and Methodius.

Golden Gate

The cathedral's south entrance is known as the Golden Gate (Zlatá brána), an elegant, triple-arched Gothic portal designed by Charles IV's favourite architect, Peter Parler.

Royal Oratory

Kings addressed their subjects from the grand, intricately crafted oratory, which appears to be woven with gnarled tree branches. This striking centrepiece exemplifies late-Gothic aesthetics.

Tomb of St John of Nepomuk

Nepomuk was a priest and religious martyr; it's said that hundreds of years after his death, when his body was exhumed, his tongue was found 'still alive'. The Church canonised him and commissioned this elaborate silver sarcophagus for his reburial. (Scientists later showed that the 'tongue' was actually brain tissue congealed in blood.)

Chapel of St Wenceslas

This is the most beautiful of the cathedral's side chapels, with walls adorned with gilded panels containing polished slabs of semiprecious stones. Murals from the early 16th century depict scenes from the life of the Czechs' patron saint, while even older frescoes show scenes from the life of Jesus. On the southern side, a small door – locked with seven locks – leads to the **coronation chamber**, where the Bohemian crown jewels are kept.

★ Top Tips

○ Try to arrive first thing in the morning, when the crowds are smaller.

○ Entry to the cathedral is included in your Prague Castle (p36) ticket.

○ For spectacular views, climb the stairway to the cathedral's tower.

✗ Take a Break

Before braving the crowds, fortify with a steaming cup of jasmine tea or a light Vietnamese meal at Malý Buddha (p50), located outside the castle complex. a short walk from the main entrance.

Top Experience 📷

Admire the Baroque Beauty of Loreta

The Loreta is a baroque pilgrimage site financed by the noble Lobkowicz family in 1626. It was designed as a replica of the Santa Casa (the home of the Virgin Mary) in the Holy Land. Legend has it that the original was carried by angels to the Italian town of Loreto as the Turks were advancing on Nazareth. The Loreta's original Counter-Reformation purpose was to wow the locals.

◎ MAP P46, B3

www.loreta.cz

Loretánské náměstí 7

adult/child 180/90Kč, photography permit 100Kč

🚋 22, 23

Santa Casa

The duplicate Santa Casa is in the centre of a courtyard complex, surrounded by cloistered arcades, churches and chapels. The interior is adorned with 17th-century frescoes and reliefs depicting the life of the Virgin Mary, as well as an ornate silver altar with a wooden effigy of Our Lady of Loreto.

Prague Sun

The eye-popping treasury boasts a star attraction – a dazzling object called the 'Prague Sun'. Studded with 6222 diamonds, it was a gift to the Loreta from Countess Ludmila of Kolowrat. In her will she wrote that the piece must be crafted from her personal collection of diamonds – wedding gifts from her third husband.

Church of the Nativity of Our Lord

Behind the Santa Casa is the Church of the Nativity of Our Lord, built in 1737 to a design by Christoph Dientzenhofer. The claustrophobic interior includes two skeletons of the Spanish saints Felicissima and Marcia, dressed in aristocratic clothing with wax masks concealing their skulls.

The Bearded Lady

At the corner of the courtyard is the unusual Chapel of Our Lady of Sorrows, featuring a crucified bearded lady. She was St Starosta, pious daughter of a Portuguese king, who promised her to the king of Sicily against her wishes. After a night of tearful prayers, she awoke with a beard, the wedding was called off, and her father had her crucified. She was later made patron saint of the needy and godforsaken.

★ **Top Tips**

o Make sure you take the worthwhile audio guide, available in several languages.

o If you'd like to take photos (no flash or tripod allowed), ask for a permit (100Kč).

✖ **Take a Break**

For a cold beer or cheap coffee, look no further than old-school Czech pub, Hostinec U Černého Vola (p51), which is opposite the Loreta.

Prague Castle & Hradčany

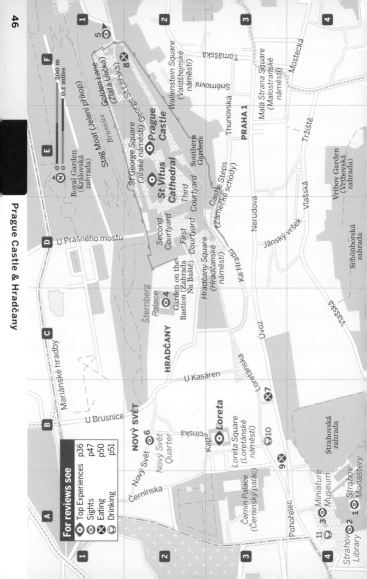

For reviews see

Top Experiences	p36
Sights	p47
Eating	p50
Drinking	p51

Mariánské hradby

U Prašného mostu

U Brusnice

NOVÝ SVĚT

Nový Svět **6**

Nový Svět Quarter

Černínská

Loreta **Loreta**

Kapucínská

Loreta Square (Loretánské náměstí)

10

9

Černín Palace (Černínský palác)

Pohořelec

Strahov Library **2** Miniature Museum

Strahov **1** Monastery

11 **3**

Strahovská zahrada

HRADČANY

Šternberg Palace

Garden on the Bastion (Zahrada Na Baště) **4**

U Kasáren

Hradčany Square (Hradčanské náměstí)

U Brusnice

Royal Garden (Královská zahrada)

Stag Moat (Jelení příkop)

Brusnice

St George Square (Jiřské náměstí)

Golden Lane (Zlatá ulička) **8**

George St (Jiřská)

Prague Castle

Wallenstein Square (Valdštejnské náměstí)

St Vitus Cathedral

Southern Gardens

Second Courtyard

First Courtyard

Third Courtyard

Castle Steps (Zámecké schody)

Ke Hradu

Tomášská

Sněmovní

Thunovská

PRAHA 1

Malá Strana Square (Malostranské náměstí)

Mostecká

Nerudova

Jánský vršek

Úvoz

Loretánská

Tržiště

Vlašská

Schönborská zahrada

Vrtbov Garden (Vrtbovská zahrada)

Vlašská

Strahovská zahrada

5

200 m
0.1 miles

N

Sights

Strahov Monastery   MONASTERY

1 MAP P46, A4

In 1140 Vladislav II founded Strahov Monastery for the Premonstratensian order. The present monastery buildings, completed in the 17th and 18th centuries, functioned until the communist government closed them down and imprisoned most of the monks; they returned in 1990. The main attraction here is the magnificent Strahov Library (p47).

Inside the main gate is the 1612 **Church of St Roch** (kostel sv Rocha), which is now an art gallery, and the **Church of the Assumption of Our Lady** (kostel Nanebevzetí Panny Marie), built in 1143 and heavily decorated in the 18th century in baroque style.

Mozart is said to have played the organ here. (www.strahovskyklaster.cz)

Strahov Library   HISTORIC BUILDING

2 MAP P46, A4

Strahov Library is the largest monastic library in the country, with two magnificent baroque halls dating from the 17th and 18th centuries. You can peek through the doors but, sadly, you can't go into the halls themselves anymore – it was found that fluctuations in humidity caused by visitors' breath were endangering the frescoes. There's also a display of historical curiosities.

The stunning interior of the two-storey-high **Philosophy Hall**

Strahov Monastery

Good 'King' Wenceslas

Thanks to British clergyman John Mason Neale, the name 'Wenceslas' is known to English speakers the world over. It was Neale who penned the popular Christmas carol 'Good King Wenceslas' in 1853. Neale was apparently inspired by the tale of a page and his master taking food and firewood to the poor on a freezing day over the Christmas holidays.

However, Neale was either mistaken or consciously exaggerating. Wenceslas ('Václav' in Czech) was never a king, but rather the duke of Bohemia who, from 925 to 929 CE, helped bring Christianity to the Czech lands. Now the Czechs' chief patron saint, his image pops up all across town, from St Vitus Cathedral to the Wenceslas Statue on (you guessed it) Wenceslas Square.

Despite his piety, Wenceslas came to an unfortunate end. He was murdered by his brother Boleslav for cosying up to neighbouring Germans.

(Filozofický sál; 1780–97) was built to fit around the carved and gilded, floor-to-ceiling walnut shelving that was rescued from another monastery in South Bohemia (access to the upper gallery is via spiral staircases concealed in the corners). The feeling of height here is accentuated by a grandiose ceiling fresco, *Mankind's Quest for True Wisdom* – the figure of Divine Providence is enthroned in the centre amid a burst of golden light, while around the edges are figures ranging from Adam and Eve to the Greek philosophers.

The lobby outside the hall contains an 18th-century **Cabinet of Curiosities,** displaying the grotesquely shrivelled remains of sharks, skates, turtles and other sea creatures. These flayed and splayed corpses were prepared by sailors, who passed them off to credulous landlubbers as 'sea monsters'. Lying on a table to the right of the entrance, along with a narwhal tusk, are two long, brown, leathery things – preserved whale penises.Another case (beside the door to the corridor) contains historical items, including a miniature coffee service made for the Habsburg empress Marie Louise in 1813 that fits into four false books.

Opposite it is the **Xyloteka** (1825), a set of book-like boxes, each one bound in the wood and bark of the tree it describes, with samples of leaves, roots, flowers and fruit inside. As you enter the corridor, look to the left to find a facsimile of the library's most prized possession, the **Strahov Evangeliary**, a 9th-century codex in a gem-studded, 12th-century binding. The corridor leads to the older but even more beautiful **Theology Hall** (Teologiský sál; 1679). The low, curved ceiling is thickly encrusted in ornate baroque stucco work, and decorated with painted cartouches depicting the theme of 'True Wisdom', which was acquired, of course, through piety – one of the mottoes that adorns the ceiling is *initio sapientiae timor domini* (the beginning of wisdom is the fear of God). (www.strahovskyk laster.cz)

Miniature Museum

MUSEUM

3 ◎ MAP P46, A4

Siberian technician Anatoly Kony-enko once manufactured tools for microsurgery, but in his spare time

he spent 7½ years crafting a pair of golden horseshoes for a flea.

See these, as well as the Lord's Prayer inscribed on a single human hair, a grasshopper clutching a violin, and a camel caravan silhouetted in the eye of a needle. Weird but fascinating. (www. muzeumminiatur)

Šternberg Palace

GALLERY

4 ◎ MAP P46, C2

The baroque Šternberg Palace is home to the National Gallery's collection of European art from ancient Greece and Rome, up to the 18th century, and includes works by Goya and Rembrandt. Fans of medieval altarpieces will be in heaven, and there are also

Theology Hall

several Rubens, some Brueghels, and a large collection of Bohemian miniatures.

Pride of the gallery is the glowing *Feast of the Rosary* by Albrecht Dürer, an artist better known for his engravings. Painted in Venice in 1505 as an altarpiece for the church of San Bartolomeo, it was brought to Prague by Rudolf II; in the background, beneath the tree on the right, is the figure of the artist himself. (www.ngprague.cz)

Kunsthalle
GALLERY

5 👁 MAP P46, F1

This brand-new, multifunctional art space near Prague Castle is the latest big development to hit the Prague arts scene. Fashioned out of the old Zenger electricity substation, a listed building, the Kunsthalle contains galleries, a bistro and shop, and hosts temporary exhibitions normally with a contemporary cut. Opened in 2022, so far some of the shows have been world class. Check the website to see what's on. (www.kunsthallepraha.org)

Nový Svět Quarter
AREA

6 👁 MAP P46, B2

In the 16th century, houses were built for castle staff in an enclave of curving cobblestone streets down the slope north of the Loreta. Today these diminutive cottages have been restored and painted in pastel shades, making the 'New World' quarter a perfect alterna-tive to the castle's crowded Golden Lane. Danish astronomer Tycho Brahe once lived at Nový Svět 1.

Eating

hOST
INTERNATIONAL €€

7 🍴 MAP P46, B3

Tucked away down a flight of steps between Úvoz and Loretánská, hOST impresses with its sleekly styled dining room, decorated with old monochrome photos, and the spectacular view from its enclosed terrace. Staff will guide you through an eclectic menu that ranges from braised lamb shank and herb-marinated duck breast, to fancy takes on Czech dishes. (www.restauranthost.cz)

Lobkowicz Palace Café
CAFE €€

8 🍴 MAP P46, F2

This cafe, housed in the 16th-century Lobkowicz Palace (p41), is the best eatery in the castle complex by an imperial mile. Try to grab one of the tables on the balconies at the back – the view over the city is superb, as are the soups, sandwiches and goulash. The coffee is good too, and service is fast and friendly. (www.lobkowicz.com)

Malý Buddha
ASIAN €

9 🍴 MAP P46, B3

Candlelight, incense and a Buddhist shrine characterise this intimate, rather incongruous Asian tearoom opposite the Swedish embassy. The menu is a blend of Asian influences, with authentic Vietnamese soups, Indian curries and Chinese rice, many of them vegetarian. The whole place smacks a little of the wild nineties, but in a good way.

Drinking

Hostinec U Černého Vola
PUB

10 MAP P46, B3

Just how this authentically rough Czech pub has managed to survive on Loretánské náměstí is as great a miracle as the flying Loreta house opposite – but it has. A spit-and-sawdust kinda place, good for experiencing the hedonistic atmosphere of the late 1980s/ early 1990s, with great beer, a raucous evening crowd, hugs from strangers, cheap pickled sausage and inflation-resistant Turkish coffee.

Klášterní Pivovar Strahov
BREWERY

11 MAP P46, A4

Dominated by two copper brewing kettles, this convivial little pub in Strahov Monastery serves up at least three or four of the seven beers its makes under the St Norbert brand. The best two are the *tmavý* (dark), a rich, tarry brew with a creamy head; and *polotmavý* (amber), a full-bodied, hoppy lager. The slightly pricey mains often use the beer as an ingredient. (www.klasterni-pivovar.cz)

Explore
Malá Strana & Petřín Hill

Almost too picturesque for its own good, the baroque district of Malá Strana (Little Quarter) tumbles down the hillside between Prague Castle and the river. The focal point here is Malá Strana Square (Malostranské náměstí), dominated by the green dome of St Nicholas Church. Petřín Hill, topped by a park and faux-but-fun Eiffel Tower, rises to the south.

The Short List

o **Petřín Hill (p54)** *Rising opposite the castle, the wooded Petřín has several attractions and is a perfect escape from the tourist crowds.*

o **Gardens of Malá Strana (p57)** *The 'secret' gardens of this neighbourhood are relaxing oases of green dotted with baroque finery.*

o **St Nicholas Church (p59)** *One of Europe's finest baroque churches dominates the eastern end of Malá Strana Square.*

o **Nerudova (p59)** *Part of the Royal Way, sloping Nerudova street climbs to the castle and is lined with tall baroque townhouses and palaces.*

Getting There & Around

🚋 Take 12, 15, 20, 22 or 23 to Malostranské náměstí, Hellichova or Újezd.

Ⓜ The closest stop is Malostranská on Line A.

Neighbourhood Map on p58

Malá Strana (p56) V_E/SHUTTERSTOCK ©

Top Experience 📷
Hike Up Petřín Hill

This 318m hill is one of Prague's largest green spaces. It's great for quiet, tree-shaded walks and fine views over the 'city of a hundred spires' from the observation deck of a highly convincing, miniature Eiffel Tower. There were once vineyards here, and a quarry that provided the stone for most of Prague's Romanesque and Gothic buildings. Take the funicular railway up the hill to add a bit of a day-trip feel.

◎ MAP P58, B3

🕐 24h

🚋 Nebozízek, Petřín

Petřín Funicular

First opened in 1891, the **Petřín Funicular Railway** (www.dpp.cz) trundles along 510m of track every 15 minutes from Újezd to the Petřín Lookout Tower, with a stop at Nebozízek.

Memorial to the Victims of Communism

Near the lower funicular station, the striking **Memorial to the Victims of Communism** sculpture shows disintegrating human figures descending a staggered slope. A bronze plaque records the terrible human toll of the communist era: 205,486 arrested; 170,938 driven into exile; 248 executed; 4500 died in prison; and 327 shot trying to escape.

Petřín Lookout Tower

Some of the best views of Prague – including, on a clear day, the Central Bohemian forests – are from the top of this 62m tower(www.muzeumprahy.cz), built in 1891 for the Prague Exposition. The Eiffel Tower lookalike has 299 steps (and a lift).

Mirror Maze

The **Mirror Maze** (www.muzeumprahy.cz), below the Lookout Tower, was also built for the 1891 Prague Exposition. The maze of distorting mirrors was based on the Prater in Vienna and is a lot of fun for kids. There's also, somewhat inexplicably, a **diorama** of the 1648 Battle of Prague.

★ Top Tips

o Before heading up the hill, stop at a bakery or supermarket to pick up a picnic. There are lots of benches and places to unfurl a blanket.

o Hiking up Petřín Hill is a pleasant alternative to the funicular and not too strenuous if you follow the winding paths.

o Ride the funicular at night for glittering views of the city.

o Instead of taking the funicular down, consider walking northward through the top of the park towards Strahov Monastery (p47).

✕ Take a Break

Restaurant Nebozízek (www.nebozizek.cz) is located halfway up Petřín Hill's funicular and is also accessible on foot. The views from the terrace are worth the climb. Café Savoy (p61), not far from the funicular base station, is great for either coffee or a light lunch.

Malá Strana & Petřín Hill Hike Up Petřín Hill

Walking Tour 🥾

Gardens of Malá Strana

The aristocrats who inhabited Malá Strana in the 17th and 18th centuries had beautiful baroque gardens created, many of which are open to the public. From April to October, whenever the sun shines, the neighbourhood's parks and gardens fill with local students toting sketchbooks, young mothers with kids, and business types relaxing on their lunch breaks. Note that from November to March, many of the parks are closed.

Start Gardens Beneath Prague Castle;
Ⓜ Malostranská

Finish Vrtbov Garden;
Ⓜ Malostranská

Length 2.5km; two hours

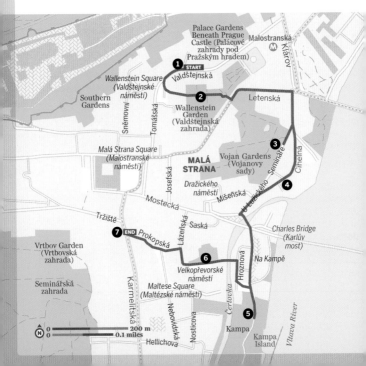

❶ Stroll the Gardens Beneath Prague Castle

The terraced **Gardens Beneath Prague Castle** (www.palacovezahrady.cz), on the steep southern slopes of the castle, date from the 17th and 18th centuries. Restored in the 1990s, they contain a Renaissance loggia with frescoes of Pompeii and a baroque portal with a sundial that cleverly catches the sunlight reflected off the water of a fountain.

❷ Admire Wallenstein Garden

The Baroque **Wallenstein Garden** is an oasis of peace amid the bustle of Malá Strana. Created for Duke Albrecht of Wallenstein in the 17th century, its finest feature is the huge loggia decorated with scenes from the Trojan Wars, flanked by an enormous fake stalactite grotto dotted with grotesque carved faces. The palace in the gardens is the upper chamber of the Czech Parliament, the Senate.

❸ Hang Out with Locals in Vojan Gardens

While less manicured than most of Malá Strana's parks, **Vojan Gardens** are a popular spot with locals who like to come here to take a breather with the kids, sit in the sun or even hold summer parties.

❹ Spot an Unusual Fountain

In the open-air plaza in front of the Franz Kafka Museum is the much-photographed David Černý sculpture, **Proudy** (www.davidcerny.cz). The quirky animatronic sculpture features two men relieving themselves into a puddle shaped like Czechia.

❺ Feel the Breeze at Kampa

Toss a Frisbee, take a load off or just watch the locals play with their dogs at the leafy riverside park known simply as **Kampa**. It's one of the city's favourite chill-out zones and hosts many events.

❻ Find Inner Peace

The **John Lennon Wall** is a memorial graffiti wall to the former Beatle who became a pacifist hero for young Czechs; his image was painted on this wall opposite the French Embassy, along with political graffiti. In 2022 it was painted over and received a huge, rather unfitting, EU-funded selfie mirror, but it's still a place young people gather.

❼ Discover a Secret Garden

The 'secret' **Vrtbov Garden** (www.vrtbovska.cz), hidden along an alley at the corner of Tržiště and Karmelitská, was built in 1720 for the Earl of Vrtba, the senior chancellor of Prague Castle. It's a formal baroque garden with baroque statues of Roman mythological figures by Matthias Braun.

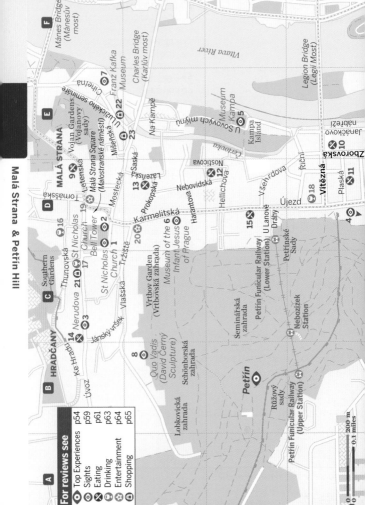

Mánes Bridge (Mánesův most)

Charles Bridge (Karlův most)

Vltava River

Legion Bridge (Legií Most)

Franz Kafka Museum 7

U lužického semináře

22

Cihelná

23

Míšeňská

Vojan Gardens (Vojanovy sady) 9

Letenská

MALÁ STRANA

Mala Strana Square (Malostranské náměstí)

Saská

Lázeňská

13

Mostecká

Prokopská

Tomášská

D

St Nicholas Church 17

19

Karmelitská

Bell Tower 2

16

Nerudova

21

St Nicholas Church 1

Thunovská

Tržiště

Vlašská

Jánský vršek

Ke Hradu 14

Uvoz

HRADČANY

Southern Gardens

Vrtbov Garden (Vrtbovská zahrada)

Museum of the Infant Jesus of Prague 6

Harantova

Quo Vadis (David Černý Sculpture) 8

Schönborská zahrada

Lobkovická zahrada

Na Kampě

Museum Kampa 5

U Sovových mlýnů

Kampa Island

Čertovka

Nosticova

Nebovidská

Hellichova

Všehrdova

Janáčkovo nábřeží

Zborovská

10

Říční

Vítězná

Plaská 11

18

Újezd

15

U Lanové Dráhy

U Lanové Dráhy

Petřín Funicular Railway (Lower Station)

Petřínské Sady

Seminářská zahrada

Nebozizek Station

Petřín

Růžový sady

Petřín Funicular Railway (Upper Station)

For reviews see
◆ Top Experiences p54
◎ Sights p59
✕ Eating p61
◖ Drinking p63
✦ Entertainment p64
▣ Shopping p65

200 m
0.1 miles

A B C D E F

1 2 3 4

Sights

St Nicholas Church

CHURCH

1 ⊙ MAP P58, D1

Malá Strana is dominated by the huge green cupola of St Nicholas Church, one of Central Europe's finest baroque buildings. (Don't confuse it with the Church of St Nicholas on Old Town Square.)

On the ceiling, Johann Kracker's 1770 *Apotheosis of St Nicholas* is Europe's largest fresco (clever *trompe l'œil* techniques have made the painting merge almost seamlessly with the architecture). (www.stnicholas.cz)

St Nicholas Church Bell Tower

TOWER

2 ⊙ MAP P58, D1

During the communist era, the bell tower of St Nicholas Church was used to spy on the nearby American embassy – on the way up you can still see a small, white, cast-iron urinal that was installed for the use of the spies. Today it provides visitors with a spectacular view over Malá Strana and Charles Bridge.

Nerudova

STREET

3 ⊙ MAP P58, C1

Following the tourist crowds downhill from the castle via Ke Hradu, you will arrive at Nerudova, architecturally the most important street in Malá Strana – most of

St Nicholas Church

ARCHITECTURE2000/ALAMY STOCK PHOTO ©

its old Renaissance facades were 'baroquefied' in the 18th century. It's named after the Czech poet Jan Neruda (famous for his short stories, *Tales of Malá Strana*), who lived at the House of the Two Suns (dům U dvou sluncú; No 47) from 1845 to 1857.

Ethnographical Museum
MUSEUM

4 ◉ MAP P58, D4

One of Prague's least-visited museums is a joy for those looking for a dash of Slavic colour. Housed in a renovated summer palace, the National Museum's ethnographic collection does a good job of providing an overview of traditional Czech folk culture and art, including music, costume, farming methods and handicrafts. It's also a venue for folk concerts and workshops demonstrating traditional crafts.

The garden cafe is an oasis of peace in summer. (www.nm.cz)

Museum Kampa
GALLERY

5 ◉ MAP P58, E3

Established by art collectors Meda and Jan Mládek and housed in a renovated mill building, this excellent gallery is devoted to 20th-century and contemporary art from Central Europe.

The highlights of the permanent exhibition are extensive collections of bronzes by cubist sculptor Otto Gutfreund and paintings by František Kupka – the most

impressive canvas is Kupka's *Cathedral,* a pleated mass of blue and red diagonals.

The museum also hosts a range of temporary exhibitions of the highest quality. (www.museum-kampa.cz)

Museum of the Infant Jesus of Prague
CHURCH

6 ◉ MAP P58, D2

The rather plain-looking Church of Our Lady Victorious (kostel Panny Marie Vítězné), built in 1613, has on its central altar a 47cm-tall waxwork figure of the baby Jesus, brought from Spain in 1628 and known as the Infant Jesus of Prague (Pražské Jezulátko, or sometimes known by its Italian name, Babino di Praga). At the back of the church is a tiny museum displaying a selection of the frocks used to dress the Infant Jesus. (www.pragjesu.cz)

Franz Kafka Museum
MUSEUM

7 ◉ MAP P58, E1

This much-hyped and slightly overpriced exhibition on the life and work of Prague's most famous literary son explores the intimate relationship between the writer and the city that shaped him, through the use of original letters, photographs, quotations, period newspapers and publications, and video and sound installations. (www.kafkamuseum.cz)

Give Me a Sign

Until numbering was introduced in the 18th century, exotic house names and signs were the only way of identifying individual Prague buildings. This practice came to a halt in 1770, when it was banned by the city councillors.

More such-named houses and signs survive on **Nerudova** (p59) than along any other Prague street. As you head downhill, look out for At the Two Suns (No 47), the Golden Horseshoe (No 34), the Three Fiddles (No 12), the Red Eagle (No 6) and the Devil (No 4). Other signs include St Wenceslas on horseback (No 34), a golden key (No 27) and a golden goblet (No 16).

Quo Vadis (David Černý Sculpture)   MONUMENT

8 ⊙ MAP P58, B2

This bronze Trabant (an East German car) on four human legs is a David Černý tribute to the 4000 East Germans who occupied the garden of the then West German embassy in 1989, before being granted political asylum and leaving their Trabants behind. You can see the sculpture through the fence behind the German embassy. To find it, head uphill along Vlašská, turn left into a children's park, and left again. (www.davidcerny.cz)

Eating

Augustine   INTERNATIONAL €€€

9 ✕ MAP P58, D1

Hidden away in the historic Augustine Hotel (check out the ceiling fresco in the bar), this sophisticated yet relaxed restaurant is well worth seeking out for a special occasion. The menu ranges from down-to-earth but delicious dishes, such as braised lamb with truffle purée, to inventive dishes built around fresh Czech produce. Dinner reservations advised. (www.augustine-restaurant.cz)

Café Savoy   EUROPEAN €€

10 ✕ MAP P58, E4

The Savoy is a beautifully restored Austrian-era cafe, with smart, suited waiting staff and a Viennese-style menu of hearty soups, salads, roast meats and schnitzels. It's also just a characterful place for a coffee-and-strudel halt after a visit to Petřín; there's also a superb wine list (ask the staff for recommendations). (http://cafesavoy.ambi.cz)

Ichnusa Botega Bistro   SARDINIAN €€

11 ✕ MAP P58, D4

'Ichnusa' is the ancient name for Sardinia, which is where owner

Walk on the Green Side

Prague is a very green city with many parks and gardens – in fact, sometimes these look more like natural countryside than city gardens.

Malá Strana is well known as the greenest part of the city centre.

Here are my top five green spaces in this attractive neighbourhood:

Valdštejnská zahrada Quiet, baroque, with nice carp and amazing views of the *hrad* (Prague Castle).

Nosticova zahrada Entering this little garden from Nosticova on a hot summer day brings an incredible feeling of calm.

Velká strahovská zahrada Some of the most spectacular views across the city are from its upper part.

Petřín Hill (p54) The atmosphere and colours here depend very much on the season.

Vojanovy sady Wonderful hidden garden next to Charles Bridge.

Recommended by
Stéphane Corbet,
owner of Orel & Friends souvenir
shop in Nerudova Street (www.orelandfriends.cz)

Antonella Pranteddu sources all of the meats, cheeses and wines he serves in this inviting, family-run affair, Eastern Europe's only Sardi resto. Exotic dishes such as *malloreddus* (a type of gnocchi), spaghetti *alla bottarga* (dried roe spaghetti) and grilled swordfish populate the menu, though (mercifully) Sardinia's donkey specialities don't feature.

U Modré Kachničky

CZECH €€€

12 MAP P58, D3

A plush 1930s-style hunting lodge hidden away on a quiet side street, 'At the Blue Duckling' is a pleasantly old-fashioned place with quiet, candlelit nooks perfect for a romantic dinner. Traditional Bohemian duck dishes are the speciality here, but the venison also comes highly recommended, and there are a couple of vegetarian choices, too. (www.umodrekachnicky.cz)

Cukrkávalimonáda

EUROPEAN €

13 MAP P58, D2

A cute little cafe-cum-bistro that combines minimalist 21st-century styling with impressive Renaissance-era painted timber roof beams, CKL offers fresh, homemade pastas, frittatas, ciabattas, salads and pancakes (sweet and savoury) by day and a slightly more sophisticated menu in the early evening. There's also a good choice of breakfasts: ham and eggs, croissants and yoghurt. The hot chocolate is a real treat. (www.cukrkavalimonada.com)

Vegan's Prague

VEGAN €€

14  MAP P58, C1

For vegans visiting the castle or Malá Strana, this clean-cut, 1st-floor restaurant is a godsend. Under heavy Renaissance beams, enjoy curries, veggie burgers, fruit dumplings and meat-and-dairy-free versions of Czech favourites, plus lots of teas, juices and organic coffees.

The tiny, one-table terrace has spellbinding views of the castle, but you can bet someone got there before you. (www.vegans prague.cz)

Luka Lu

BALKAN €€

15  MAP P58, D3

Possibly Prague's most colourful restaurant is this south Slav affair specialising in Balkan grilled meat and other dishes from Serbia and the former Yugoslavia. Brightly coloured and full of tasteful knick-knacks throughout, this is a fun place for lunch, especially in summer when the courtyard out back is open. Many a famous Czech face has left a tip here. (www.lukalu.cz)

Drinking

U Hrocha

BEER HALL

16  MAP P58, D1

Just around the corner from the British Embassy, this old Malá Strana boozer hasn't changed

U Modré Kachničky

Kafka: Digging Deeper

'Someone must have been telling lies about Josef K, for without having done anything wrong, he was arrested one fine morning' – that opening line in Franz Kafka's *The Trial* (1925) is widely considered to be among the greatest in world literature. The words are also a testament to Prague's disorientating nature, and in the writer's home city it's hard not to be moved by his genius. Of course, it's simple to pay tribute to Kafka by visiting his birthplace or grave, but true fans will want to use the opportunity to delve more into the novelist's complex relationship with Prague, which he complained was small and claustrophobic but got under your skin. The **Franz Kafka Museum** (p60) is just the place.

much since the grotty days of the worker's republic, and is still serving its Urquell and basic soak-up food at simple wooden benches. It's normally inhabited by locals, so who knows, you might get to meet His Majesty's ambassador enjoying a night on the tiles here.

Hostinec U Kocoura PUB

 17 MAP P58, C1

A traditional Malá Strana local on the Royal Way, 'The Tomcat' still enjoys its reputation as a former favourite of late president Havel, and still manages to pull in a mostly Czech crowd despite being in the heart of a heavily touristed area (the gruff service may be the key). It has relatively inexpensive beer for this part of town.

Klub Újezd BAR

18 MAP P58, D4

Klub Újezd is one of Prague's many 'alternative' bars, spread over

three floors (DJs in the cellar, and a cafe upstairs) and filled with a fascinating collection of original art and weird wrought-iron sculptures. Clamber onto a two-tonne bar stool in the grungy street-level bar and sip on a beer beneath a scaly, fire-breathing sea monster. (www.klubujezd.cz)

Entertainment

Malostranská Beseda LIVE MUSIC

19 MAP P58, D1

A legendary Prague venue, Malá Strana's four-storey entertainment palace boasts a fabled music club on the 2nd floor, with a lively roster of Czech acts old and new, famous and 'keep-your-day-job'. There's also a low-key art gallery on the top floor, a bar and restaurant on the ground floor, and a big beer hall in the basement. (www.malostranska-beseda.cz)

U Malého Glena

LIVE MUSIC

20 ⭐ MAP P58, D2

American-owned 'Little Glen's' has been around since 1995 and is *the* venue for hard-swinging local jazz or blues bands who play every night in the cramped and steamy stone-vaulted cellar. There are Sunday-night jam sessions where amateurs are welcome (as long as you're good!) – it's a small venue, so get here early if you want to see as well as hear the band. (www.malyglen.cz)

Shopping

Orel & Friends

ARTS & CRAFTS

21 🔒 MAP P58, C1

Forget the cannabis lollipops and Russian matrioshka dolls, Orel & Friends stocks only top-notch, authentic souvenirs, made across Czechia and gathered in this small shop in Nerudova. Choose from Unesco-listed *modrotisk* (blue print) tablecloths, handmade glass Christmas decorations, unique notebooks individualised by local artists and lots of ceramics.

The French owner has a bit of a thing about the Czechs' coloured trail markers and produces a range of souvenirs featuring these striped signs that can be found on trees and fence posts across the land. (www.orelandfriends.cz)

Shakespeare & Sons

BOOKS

22 🔒 MAP P58, E1

Though its shelves groan with a formidable range of literature in English, French and German, this is more than just a bookshop (with Prague's best range of titles on Eastern European history) – it's also a congenial literary hang-out with knowledgeable staff, occasional author events and a cool downstairs space for sitting and reading. (www.shakes.cz)

Artěl

DESIGN

23 🔒 MAP P58, E2

Traditional Bohemian glass-making meets modern design in this stylish shop founded by US designer Karen Feldman. In addition to hand-blown designer crystal, you can find a range of vintage and modern items of Czech design, from jewellery and ceramics to toys and stationery. (www.artelglass.com)

Malá Strana & Petřín Hill Shopping

Walking Tour 🚶

Beer & Culture in Smíchov

Standing in contrast to the fairy-tale historic sphere of castles and royal gardens, working-class Smíchov is a mainly industrial district on the Vltava's western bank. With its vibrant contemporary-art scene and unpretentious bars, the slightly gritty neighbourhood offers an authentic taste of Czech life, though its character is slowly changing.

Start Jazz Dock;
🚊 Arbesovo náměstí
Finish Meet Factory;
🚊 Lihovar
Length 6.3km; three hours

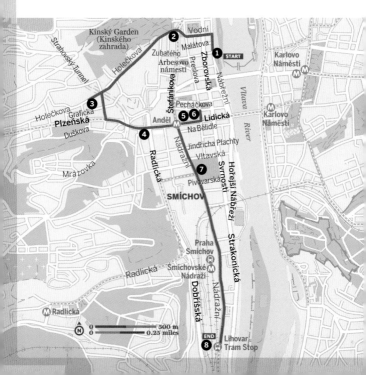

❶ Jazz on the River

Start at **Jazz Dock** (www.jazzdock.cz), Smíchov's well-known riverside jazz venue for some food and drinks. Keep this place in mind to return to later in the evening for a show. Most Prague jazz clubs are cellar affairs; Jazz Dock has a lighter, contemporary decor and a romantic view over the Vltava.

❷ Avant-Garde Theatre at Švandovo Divadlo

Walk north and then west along Vodní to find the funky **Švandovo Divadlo** (www.svandovodivadlo.cz). This is a popular, avant-garde cinema that stages many shows with English subtitles. It also hosts art exhibits and events.

❸ Contemporary Art at Futura

Follow busy Holečkova southwest a few blocks to the **Futura Gallery** (www.futuraproject.cz), home to a famous, irreverent art installation by David Černý called *Brown-nosers* (2003). Climb up and stick your head inside the statue's backside to see a video of former Czech president Václav Klaus and the National Gallery's director feeding each other baby food.

❹ Czech Food at Zlatý Klas

With the cultural part of the tour out of the way, continue south and east towards a cosy Pilsner-Urquell pub restaurant called **Zlatý Klas** (www.zlatyklas.cz) to begin the drinking part. This place is beloved both for its hearty, well-prepared Czech cuisine and well-preserved Pilsner-Urquell beer, stored in large tanks.

❺ Modern Take on a Czech Pub

Further east, along the same street, **Andělský Pivovar** (www.andelskypivovar.cz) offers a welcome contrast to Smíchov's more traditional pubs, like Zlatý Klas. This is an airy, thoroughly renovated space with its own craft beers.

❻ Drinking at the 'Bulldog'

Just around the corner, nip in for a quick one at the classic sports bar, **Hospoda U Buldoka** (www.ubuldoka.cz). There's a decadent drink-till-you-drop vibe here.

❼ Another Round at Staropramen Brewery

Head south on Nádražní a few blocks to sample beer from Prague's own Staropramen Brewery. **Na Verandách** (www.phnaverandach.cz) is housed on the brewery grounds and promises the freshest pour you can find. It's also great for food if you haven't eaten yet.

❽ 'MeetFactory' Meet-Ups

Walk south along Nádražní several blocks (take the tram to stop Lihovar to save time) to find **MeetFactory** (www.meetfactory.cz), artist David Černý's cutting-edge venue for films, concerts, theatrical performances and art installations.

Explore ✦
Jewish Museum & Josefov

Peaceful Josefov is the site of the former Jewish ghetto – the physical, cultural and spiritual home to the city's Jewish population for nearly 800 years. While many Jews left the quarter when it was renovated in the early 20th century (and tens of thousands were killed in the Holocaust), the surviving synagogues and cemetery make up the popular Jewish Museum.

The Short List

◦ **Old Jewish Cemetery (p72)** *Highly atmospheric spot with its crooked gravestones and Hebrew-inscribed tombs.*

◦ **Old-New Synagogue (p75)** *The oldest working synagogue on the continent is wreathed in myths.*

◦ **Spanish Synagogue (p71)** *The most beautiful of the Josefov synagogues houses a museum.*

◦ **Gurmet Pasáž Dlouhá (p81)** *Artisan fare galore at this food court in an old art-deco arcade.*

◦ **Convent of St Agnes (p75)** *Home to a stunning collection of medieval and early Renaissance art.*

Getting There & Around

🚊 Lines 2, 17, 18 to Staroměstská; Lines 6, 8, 15, 26 to Dlouhá třída.

Ⓜ Line A to Staroměstská.

Neighbourhood Map on p74

Klaus Synagogue (p71) TATIANA DIUYBANOVA/SHUTTERSTOCK ©

Top Experience 📷
Gain Insight at the Jewish Museum

Prague's Jewish Museum is among the city's most visited sights. It was established in 1906 to preserve artefacts from the quarter after it was razed and renovated in the late-19th and early-20th centuries. Highlights include the Pinkas Synagogue and its memorial to Czech and Moravian Jews killed in the Holocaust.

◎ MAP P74, B3

Židovské muzeum Praha

www.jewishmuseum.cz

🕓 9am-6pm Sun-Fri Apr-Oct, to 4.30pm Nov-Mar

Ⓜ Staroměstská

Klaus Synagogue & Ceremonial Hall

Both the baroque **Klaus Synagogue** (www.jewishmuseum.cz) and the nearby **Ceremonial Hall** contain exhibits on Jewish health and burial traditions.

Maisel Synagogue

Mordechai Maisel was mayor of the Jewish quarter under the liberal rule of Emperor Rudolf II during the 16th century. He was also the richest man in Prague, and in addition to various public works, he paid for this **synagogue** for his private use. It houses rotating exhibitions.

Pinkas Synagogue

Built in 1535, this **synagogue** was used for worship until 1941. It's now a moving Holocaust memorial, its walls inscribed with the names, birthdates and dates of disappearance of 77,297 Czech Jews. See a poignant exhibition of drawings made by children held at the Terezín concentration camp during WWII.

Spanish Synagogue

Considered the most beautiful of the museum's synagogues, this 19th-century Moorish-style **building** boasts an ornate interior and an exhibition on recent Jewish history.

★ Top Tips

○ Queues for tickets are generally shortest at the Spanish Synagogue.

○ Visit the Old Jewish Cemetery early or late in order to find it at its most peaceful.

○ Men must cover their heads before entering the Old-New Synagogue. Bring a hat or buy a paper yarmulke at the entrance.

✖ Take a Break

For a good pint of beer in the vicinity of the Spanish Synagogue, head to corner pub V Kolkovně (p79).

Top Experience 📷
Wander through the Old Jewish Cemetery

City authorities once insisted that deceased Jews be interred only here – nowhere else – so by the time this cemetery stopped taking new burials in 1787, it was full to bursting. Today it holds more than 12,000 tombstones, though many more than that are buried here. Be aware that conditions at this popular attraction sometimes feel almost as crowded for the living as for the dead.

◎ **MAP P74, B3**

Starý židovský hřbitov

www.jewishmuseum.cz

Pinkas Synagogue, Široká 3

included in admission to Prague Jewish Museum

Ⓜ Staroměstská

Rabbi Loew's Tomb

Sometimes called 'the Jewish hero of the Czechs', Rabbi Judah Loew ben Bezalel (1525–1609) was a respected scholar and the chief rabbi of Bohemia in the 16th century. Perhaps more importantly to Czech people, he's part of a legend surrounding the creation of the Golem, a creature he supposedly built from clay to protect the Jewish people living in Prague's ghetto.

Mordechai Maisel's Tomb

This tomb honours a philanthropist with some incredibly deep pockets. In addition to serving as a Jewish leader in the 16th century, Maisel was the city's wealthiest citizen. He paid for the construction of new buildings in the ghetto, had the roads paved, commissioned the Maisel Synagogue (p71) for his own private use and even lent money to Emperor Rudolf II.

David Gans' Tomb

A noted German historian and astronomer, Gans came to Prague in part to hear the lectures of Rabbi Loew. He's perhaps most famous for his association with Tycho Brahe, who asked Gans to translate the Alphonsine Tables from Hebrew to German.

Joseph Solomon Delmedigo's Tomb

Another impressive Jewish intellectual represented in the cemetery is Joseph Solomon Delmedigo, who was both a physician and a philosopher. He studied and worked all over Europe before finally settling in Prague in 1648 to write various scientific texts.

★ **Top Tips**

○ Entry to the cemetery is included in the general Jewish Museum admission ticket.

○ Arrive early as the cemetery gets increasingly busy as the day goes on.

○ Remember that you're in a cemetery – always be careful where you step.

✕ **Take a Break**

Stylish Mistral Café (p79) is a short walk from the cemetery and is great for coffee or a light meal.

Also nearby is **U Rudolfina** (www.urudolfina.cz), a down-to-earth local pub with some of the city's best Pilsner Urquell.

For reviews see

◎ Top Experiences — p70
◉ Sights — p75
✕ Eating — p77
◯ Drinking — p80
◒ Entertainment — p81
◉ Shopping — p81

0 — 0.1 miles
0 — 200 m

Vltava River

Čech Bridge (Čechův most)

Intercontinental Hotel

Dvořákovo nábřeží

17 listopadu

Museum of Decorative Arts

Rudolfinum

◎ 3
◎ 16

Jan Palach Square (náměstí Jana Palacha)

Staroměstská

Křižovnická

✕ 10

Wittmann Tours (300m)

Valentinská

Kaprova

Žatecká

Kaprova

Maiselova

Široká

Pařížská

◎ Prague Jewish Museum

✕ 1

Červená

Old-New Synagogue

◎ Old Jewish Cemetery

◎ 4

PRAHA 1

Eliška Krásnohorské

Dušní

JOSEFOV

Bílkova

U Milosrdných

Kozí

◎ 6

Franz Kafka Monument

◎ 5

✕ 9

V Kolkovně

Vězeňská

15 ◎

11 ✕

13 ◎

20 ◉

Dušní

Salvátorská

Pařížská

Jáchymova

Jáchymova

Old Town Square (Staroměstské náměstí)

Dlouhá

Týnská ulička

Týnská

Týn Courtyard (Týnský dvůr)

Malá Štupartsk

Masná

Masná

Masná

Rybná

Rybná

Prague Wheelchair Users Organisation

Benediktská

Kotva

Jakubská

Kolacherie (85m)

Dlouhá

Rybná

19 ✕

8 ✕

17 ✕

12 ◉

18 ◉

7 ✕

Hastalská

Haštalské náměstí

Rámová

U obecního dvora

14 ✕

Convent of St Agnes

◎ 2

Sights

Old-New Synagogue

SYNAGOGUE

1 ◉ MAP P74, B3

Completed around 1270, this is Europe's oldest working synagogue and one of Prague's earliest Gothic buildings. You step down into it because it pre-dates the raising of Staré Město's street level in medieval times to guard against floods. Men must cover their heads (bring a hat or take one of the paper yarmulkes handed out at the entrance). Although it's one of the seven Jewish monuments that make up the Prague Jewish Museum, entry isn't included in the museum's general admission ticket. Around the central chamber are an entry hall, a winter prayer hall and the room from which women watch the men-only services. The interior, with a pulpit surrounded by a 15th-century wrought-iron grill, looks much as it would have 500 years ago. On the eastern wall is the Holy Ark that holds the Torah scrolls. In a glass case at the rear, little light bulbs beside the names of the prominent deceased are lit on their death days. (www.jewishmuseum.cz)

Convent of St Agnes

GALLERY

2 ◉ MAP P74, E1

In the northeastern corner of Staré Město is the former Convent of St Agnes, Prague's oldest surviving Gothic building.

The 1st-floor rooms hold the National Gallery's permanent

Old New Synagogue

TATIANA DUUVBANOVA/SHUTTERSTOCK ©

Jewish-Themed Tours

Wittmann Tours (Map p74; www.wittmann-tours.com) offers private, three-hour walking tours of Jewish Prague as well as guided excursions to Terezin, Auschwitz and other places of interest to Jewish heritage. Choose and book tours online. Tour times and meet-up places are flexible and negotiable.

collection of medieval and early Renaissance art (1200–1550) from Bohemia and Central Europe, a treasure house of glowing Gothic altar paintings and religious sculptures.

In 1234 the Franciscan Order of the Poor Clares was founded by Přemyslid king, Wenceslas I, who made his sister Anežka (Agnes) the first abbess of the convent. In the 16th century the convent was handed over to the Dominicans, and after Joseph II dissolved the monasteries, it became a squatters' paradise.

It is only since the 1980s that the complex has been restored and renovated. Agnes was beatified in the 19th century and, with hardly accidental timing, Pope John Paul II canonised her as St Agnes of Bohemia just weeks before the revolutionary events of November 1989. In addition to the art gallery and the 13th-century cloister, you can visit the French

Gothic **Church of the Holy Saviour**, which contains the tombs of St Agnes and Queen Cunegund. Alongside this is the smaller **Church of St Francis**, where Wenceslas I is buried. The gallery is wheelchair-accessible, and the cloister has a tactile presentation of 12 casts of medieval sculptures with explanatory text in Braille. (www.ngprague.cz)

Rudolfinum   HISTORIC BUILDING

3 ◎ MAP P74, A3

Presiding over Jan Palach Square (náměstí Jana Palacha) is the Rudolfinum, home to the Czech Philharmonic Orchestra (Česká filharmonie). This and the National Theatre, both designed by architects Josef Schulz and Josef Zítek, are considered Prague's finest neo-Renaissance buildings. Completed in 1884, the Rudolfinum served as the seat of the Czechoslovak Parliament between the wars, and as administrative offices of the occupying Nazis during WWII. The impressive Dvořák Hall (p81), its stage dominated by a vast organ, is one of the main concert venues for the **Prague Spring** festival. The northern part of the complex houses the **Galerie Rudolfinum** (www.galerierudolfinum. cz). (www.rudolfinum.cz)

Museum of Decorative Arts   MUSEUM

4 ◎ MAP P74, A3

This museum opened in 1900 as part of a European movement to encourage a return to the aesthetic values sacrificed to the Industrial Revolution. Once a graceful old museum packed with Czech glass, furniture and period clothing, the whole thing was completely renovated several years ago. (www.upm.cz)

Franz Kafka Monument
MONUMENT

 5 MAP P74, C3

Commissioned by Prague's Franz Kafka Society in 2003, Jaroslav Róna's unusual sculpture of a mini-Kafka riding on the shoulders of a giant empty suit was based on the writer's *Description of a Struggle,* in which the author explores a fantasy landscape from the shoulders of 'an acquaintance' (who may be another aspect of the author's personality).

Eating

Field
CZECH €€€

 6 MAP P74, D1

This Michelin-starred restaurant is unfussy and fun. The decor is an amusing art-meets-agriculture blend of never-used farmyard implements and minimalist chic, while the chef creates painterly presentations from local produce and freshly foraged herbs and flowers. You'll have to book some weeks in advance. (www.fieldrestaurant.cz)

La Bottega Bistroteka
ITALIAN €€€

 7 MAP P74, F2

You'll find smart and snappy service at this stylish deli-cum-bistro, where the menu makes the most of all that delicious Italian produce artfully arranged on the counter; the beef-cheek cannelloni with parmesan sauce and fava beans, for example, is just exquisite. It's best to book, but you can often get a walk-in table at lunchtime. (www.bistroteka.cz)

Lokál
CZECH €€

 8 MAP P74, F2

Take a classic Czech beer hall (albeit with cool retro-modern styling), excellent *tankové pivo* (tanked

The Myths of Golem City

Tales of golems, or servants created from clay, date back to early Judaism. However, the most famous such mythical creature belonged to 16th-century Prague's Rabbi Loew, of the **Old-New Synagogue** (p75). Loew is said to have used mud from the Vltava's banks to create a golem to protect the Prague ghetto. However, left alone one Sabbath, the creature ran amok and Rabbi Loew was forced to rush out of a service and remove the magic talisman that kept it moving. He then carried the lifeless body into the synagogue's attic, where some insist it remains.

Jewish Prague

Jews have been part of Prague for as long as the city has existed, though their status has ebbed and flowed. For centuries, Jews were restricted to living in a small corner of the Old Town (today's Josefov). Some periods brought terror and pogroms, while others – the early 17th century – brought prosperity. In the 19th century, Jews were allowed to live outside their ghetto, but a century later most were murdered by the occupying Nazis.

Early Oppression

Jews began living in Prague in the 10th century, and by the 11th century the city was one of Europe's most important Jewish centres. The Crusades marked the start of the Jews' plight as the city's oldest synagogue was burned to the ground. By the end of the 12th century, they lost many rights; soon they were forced into a walled ghetto. For years, Jews remained third-class citizens while emperors and the nobility argued over who should be in charge of Jewish affairs.

The Golden Age

The mid-16th to early-17th century is considered the golden age of Jewish history. Emperor Rudolf II (r 1576–1612) worked closely with Mayor Mordechai Maisel (1528–1601), at the time the wealthiest man in Prague. The community was led in spirit by noted mystic and Talmudic scholar Rabbi Loew (1525–1609). Emancipation came in the 18th century under Habsburg Emperor Josef II. In 1848 Jews won the right of abode, meaning they could live where they wanted. The ghetto's walls were torn down and the Jewish quarter was renamed Josefov (to honour Josef II). At the end of the 19th century, the area was levelled and rebuilt in art-nouveau splendour.

Destruction & Preservation

The Jewish community was largely destroyed by the Nazis in WWII, and only a few thousand Jews remain. One historic irony is that many of the Jewish Museum's holdings come from *shtetls* (Jewish villages) liquidated by the Nazis.

Pilsner-Urquell), a daily-changing menu of traditional Bohemian dishes and throw in some unusually smiling, efficient, friendly service, and you have Lokál. The combination has been so successful that the place is always busy and the concept has been copied across Prague in recent years. (www.lokal-dlouha.ambi.cz)

V Kolkovně
CZECH €€

9 MAP P74, D3

Operated by the Pilsner Urquell Brewery, V Kolkovně is a stylish, modern take on the traditional Prague pub, with decor by Czech designers and fancier versions of classic Czech dishes such as goulash, roast duck and beef sirloin, as well as the odd intruder such as salmon and lamb chops. All washed down with an unsurpassed Urquell beer, of course. (www.vkolkovne.cz)

Mistral Café
BISTRO €

10 MAP P74, A4

This peaceful bistro, done out in pale stone, bleached birchwood and potted shrubs, is hiding in plain sight, on a busy corner just a couple of blocks from Old Town Square.

The menu features breakfast items as well as sandwiches and healthy bowls, making it an ideal choice for a coffee, snack or light meal. (www.mistralcafe.cz)

Bakeshop Praha
BAKERY €

11 MAP P74, D3

This fantastic bakery sells some of the best bread in the city, along with pastries, cakes and takeaway sandwiches, wraps, salads and quiches. Their focus is on traditional recipes, high-quality ingredients and a love of fresh food. Be prepared to queue. It gets very busy at lunchtime. (www.bakeshop.cz)

Foodie Favourites on a Budget

Lod Pivovar ('Brewery Boat') Find this ship-based microbrewery on the Vltava River below Štefánik Bridge.

It serves unique craft beers hopped with Czech 'green gold': the country's fabled Saaz hops. Don't miss sampling the *nakladaný hermelín* (marinated cheese). It's similar to French camembert and served with home-baked bread.

Perníčkův sen (p99) This family-owned, Old Town bakery is the only place in Prague where you can buy and taste a traditional Bohemian *sakrajda* roll: gingerbread strudel stuffed with plum jam and walnuts.

Kolacherie (www.kolacherie.cz) Forget those phony *trdelník* (chimney-cake) stands you see around town. These fresh-baked *koláče* (soft, round pastries, flavoured with fruit or poppy seeds) are as Czech as it gets.

Recommended by **Eva Brejlová**, *food tour leader for Eating Prague* (www.eatingeurope.com/prague)

Drinking

Bokovka
WINE BAR

12 MAP P74, F2

Founded by a syndicate of oenophiles, including film directors Jan Hřebejk and David Ondříček, Bokovka has moved from its original New Town location to this hidden courtyard. Look for the red-wine-droplet sign: the door is opposite it on the right. The crumbling, atmospheric cellar bar is a great place to sample the best of Czech wines. The bar is named after the movie *Sideways* (*Bokovka* in Czech), which is set in Californian vineyards. (www.bokovka.com)

Tretter's New York Bar
BAR

13 MAP P74, D3

This sultry 1930s Manhattan-style cocktail bar harks back to swisher times when people went out for nightcaps – and when the drinks were stiff and properly made. Regularly rated as one of the capital's top bars, Tretter's attracts a stylish crowd and has prices to match. Book your table in advance. (www.bar-tretters.cz)

James Joyce
PUB

14 MAP P74, E2

Join English speakers at this Prague original, a friendly pub that boasts something rarely seen in the city's bars: an open fire. Toast your toes while sipping a pricey Guinness, or downing the all-day Irish breakfast fry, including

Clonakilty black pudding. There's cricket and rugby on TV and a good 'ole pub quiz on Mondays. (www.jamesjoyceprague.cz)

Kozička
BAR

15 MAP P74, D3

The 'Little Goat' is a buzzing, red-brick basement bar decorated with steel goat sculptures, serving Krušovice on tap and slightly pricey Czech pub food. It fills up later in the evening with a mix of tourists and students. The late closing time makes a civilised setting in which to finish off a late-night session. (www.kozicka.cz)

Entertainment

Dvořák Hall
CONCERT VENUE

16 MAP P74, A3

The Dvořák Hall in the neo-Renaissance Rudolfinum (p76) is home to the world-renowned Czech Philharmonic Orchestra. Sit back and be impressed by some of the best classical musicians in Prague. (www.ceskafilharmonie.cz)

Roxy
LIVE MUSIC

17 MAP P74, F2

Set in the ramshackle shell of an art-deco cinema, the legendary Roxy has nurtured the more independent end of Prague's club spectrum for almost three decades. This is the place to see Czechia's top DJs, and on the 1st floor is NoD, an 'experimental space' that stages drama, dance, cinema and live music. (www.roxy.cz)

Shopping

Gurmet Pasáž Dlouhá
FOOD & DRINKS

18 MAP P74, F2

Prague's foodie scene centres on this upmarket, art-deco arcade dedicated to fine food. As well as eateries such as **Naše Maso** (www.nasemaso.cz) and **Banh Mi Makers** (www.banhmimakers.com), you'll find shops selling Czech open-faced sandwiches and Polish-style baguettes.

Talacko
MUSIC

19 MAP P74, E2

Pick up the score for Mozart's *Don Giovanni* or Dvořák's *New World Symphony* at this eclectic sheet-music shop. Or you might enjoy some popular music favourites – how about *101 Beatles Songs for Buskers?* (www.talacko.cz)

Klára Nademlýnská
FASHION & ACCESSORIES

20 MAP P74, D3

Klára Nademlýnská is one of the country's top fashion designers, having trained in Prague and worked for almost a decade in Paris. Her clothes are characterised by clean lines, simple styling and quality materials, and cover the spectrum from swimwear to evening wear via jeans. (www.klaranademlynska.cz)

Explore ◎

Old Town Square & Staré Město

Staré Město (Old Town), with its evocative medieval square, maze of alleyways and quirky sights like the Astronomical Clock, is the beating heart of the historic centre. Its origins date back to the 10th century. A thousand years later, it's as alive as ever, and surprisingly little changed by time.

The Short List

○ **Old Town Square (p84)** Prague's medieval centrepiece is a must-see for every visitor.

○ **Charles Bridge (p86)** Prague's 14th-century Gothic bridge that spans the River Vltava with an open-air gallery of baroque statuary.

○ **Municipal House (p91)** One of Europe's most exuberant art-nouveau buildings containing highly decorative restaurants, a concert hall and various salons.

○ **Astronomical Clock (p85)** The Old Town's medieval masterpiece puts on an automaton show on the hour, every hour.

○ **Estates Theatre (p98)** Grand old theatre where Mozart himself premiered Don Giovanni to an appreciative Prague audience.

Getting There & Around

🚋 Lines 2, 17 and 18 run to Staroměstská; Lines 6, 8, 15 and 26 stop at Dlouhá třída.

Ⓜ Take Line A to Staroměstská (the closest stop to Old Town Square) or Line A or B to Můstek.

Neighbourhood Map on p90

Old Town Square (p84) NG-SPACETIME/SHUTTERSTOCK ©

Top Experience 📸

Gather in the Old Town Square

*Laid with cobblestones and surrounded by spec-
tacular baroque churches, soaring spires, candy-
coloured buildings and a rococo palace, Old Town
Square is an architectural smorgasbord and a
photographer's delight. While the Astronomical
Clock – a mechanical marvel that still chimes on
the hour – is more than 600 years old, many of
the structures in the square are even older.*

◎ MAP P90, D1

Staroměstské náměstí

admission free

Ⓜ Staroměstská

Astronomical Clock

Built in 1490 by a master clockmaker named Hanuš, the **Astronomical Clock** was a scientific feat in its day – even after various renovations, it remains a paradigm of antique technology. On the hour (from 9am to 9pm), crowds gather below for its quaint visual display.

Old Town Hall Clock Tower

Old Town Hall, dating from 1338, has more to offer than its clock. Climb (or take the lift) up the **clock tower** (www.prague.eu) for privileged views over Old Town Square and the historic city centre.

Jan Hus & Mary

Two religious statues stand near the centre of the square. Ladislav Šaloun's brooding art-nouveau Jan Hus was unveiled on 6 July 1915, the 500th anniversary of Hus' death at the stake. The slender Marian Column was added only in 2020 to replace a 17th-century baroque statue that was pulled down in 1918 by anti-Habsburg nationalists.

Church of Our Lady Before Týn

Straight out of a 15th-century fairy tale, the spiky, spooky Gothic spires of **Church of Our Lady Before Týn** (www.tyn.cz), aka Týn Church, are an unmistakable Old Town landmark. It also houses the tomb of Tycho Brahe.

Church of St Nicholas

This pretty baroque **monastery** (www.svmikulas .cz) is relatively new – finished in 1735, it replaced a Gothic church built here in the late 13th century. After several incarnations, it now serves as a Czechoslovak Hussite church and a classical-concert venue.

★ **Top Tips**

o For the best views of the Astronomical Clock, come to the 9am or 10am show. Arrive a few minutes before the hour.

o Look for lively food and craft stalls in Old Town Square around major holidays such as Christmas and Easter.

o Climb (or take the lift) up the clock tower for spectacular views over Old Town Square. Earlier is better.

o The most romantic time to visit the square is after dark, when the medieval buildings are beautifully illuminated.

✕ **Take a Break**

Enjoy a healthy meal at the vegetarian restaurant Maitrea (p96), just steps from the square. Otherwise there are countless touristy cafes on the square itself.

Top Experience 📷
Walk Across Iconic Charles Bridge

You know a historic landmark is special when even the crowds hardly dull its magnificence. So it is with Charles Bridge, Prague's signature monument. Commissioned in 1357, the massive, 520m-long stone bridge was the only link across the Vltava River between Prague Castle and the Old Town until 1741. It's particularly awe-inspiring at dawn in winter when few visitors are around.

◎ MAP P90, A2

Karlův most

⏲ 24hr

🚊 2, 17, 18 to Karlovy lázně, 1, 5, 7, 12, 15, 20, 22, 25 to Malostranské náměstí

View from the Old Town Bridge Tower

Perched at the eastern end of Charles Bridge, the elegant late-14th-century **Old Town Bridge Tower** (www.prague.eu) was built not only as a fortification but also as a triumphal arch marking the entrance to the Old Town. Head upstairs for the dramatic view over the crowded bridge.

Saintly Statues

The first monument erected on the bridge was the crucifix near the eastern end, in 1657. The first statue – the Jesuits' 1683 tribute to St John of Nepomuk – inspired other Catholic orders, and over the next 30 years a score more went up. Today most are copies, but a few of the originals can be seen at the Brick Gate & Casements (p125) at the Vyšehrad Citadel.

Rubbing the Statue of St John of Nepomuk

The most famous statue is that of St John of Nepomuk, on the bridge's northern side, about halfway across. According to legend, Wenceslas IV had him thrown off the bridge in 1393 for refusing to divulge the queen's confessions (he was her priest). Tradition says that if you rub the bronze plaque, you will one day return to Prague.

Charles Bridge Museum

Examine the history of the Vltava's most famous crossing at the **Charles Bridge Museum** (www.charlesbridgemuseum.com), located near the bridge's Old Town entrance. When you learn about the bridge's tumultuous 650-year history, including at least two perilous encounters with floods, you'll be surprised it's still standing.

★ Top Tips

○ Visit the bridge at sunrise to beat the crowds.

○ Keep your valuables close at hand: pickpockets lurk here, especially in summer.

○ Plan to cross the bridge at least twice – once towards the castle and once away from it.

○ Dawn is the ideal time for photos and, in winter, if it starts snowing, head for the bridge to capture some unforgettable images.

✕ Take a Break

Not far from the entrance to the Old Town side of the bridge, the student cafe of Café Kampus (p97) is a great place to relax over a coffee or beer.

Splurge on a gourmet meal paired with Czech wine at V Zátiší (p95), close to the Old Town side of the bridge.

Walking Tour 🚶

Kafka's Prague

*'This narrow circle encompasses my entire life',
Franz Kafka (1883–1924) once said, drawing an
outline around Prague's Old Town. While an exag-
geration (he travelled and died abroad), Prague is
a constant, unspoken presence in Kafka's writing,
and this walk through the Old Town passes some
of his regular haunts.*

Start Náměstí Republiky;
Ⓜ Náměstí Republiky

Finish Hotel
Intercontinental
Ⓜ Staroměstská

Length 2km; 40 minutes

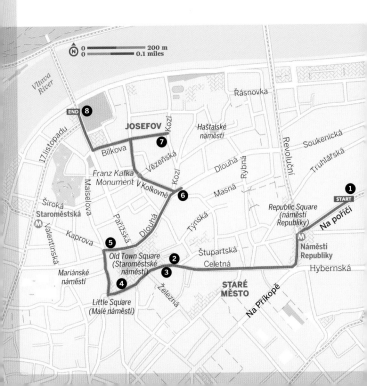

❶ Worker's Accident Insurance Company

Kafka's fiction was informed by his mundane day job as an insurance clerk – he worked for 14 years (1908–22) at the Worker's Accident Insurance Company at Na poříčí 7. His walk home passed the **Powder Gate** (p92) and the newly built **Municipal House** (p91).

❷ House of the Three Kings

Just before Old Town Square, at Celetná 3, is the House of the Three Kings, where the Kafkas lived from 1896 to 1907. Franz's room, overlooking the **Church of Our Lady Before Týn** (p85), is where he wrote his first story.

❸ Sixt House

Across Celetná, the Sixt House was an earlier childhood home (1888–89). Nearby, at Staroměstské náměstí 17, is **At the Unicorn** (U Jednorožce) – home to Berta Fanta, who hosted literary salons for thinkers of the day, including Kafka and a young Albert Einstein.

❹ House of the Minute

The **House of the Minute** (dům U minuty), the Renaissance corner building attached to the Old Town Hall, was where Franz lived as a young boy (1889–96). He later re-called being dragged to his school in Masná street by the family cook.

❺ Kafka's Birthplace

Just west of the **Church of St Nicholas** (p85) is Kafka's birthplace, marked by a bust of him at náměstí Franze Kafky 3 (formerly U Radnice 5). All that remains of the original house is the stone portal.

❻ Kafka's Bachelor Pad

Despite several fraught love affairs, Kafka never married and lived mostly with his parents. One of his few **bachelor flats** can be found at Dlouhá 16.

❼ Bílkova Apartment

Continuing north past the **Franz Kafka Monument** (p77), you'll come to another of Kafka's temporary apartments at Bílkova 22. In 1914 he began *The Trial* here.

❽ Former Hotel Intercontinental

Head west to Pařížská and north toward the river. On the grounds of the **former Hotel Intercontinental** (Pařížská 30), another Kafka family apartment (1907–13) once stood. Here, Franz wrote his Oedipal short story 'The Judgment' (1912), and began *Metamorphosis*, about a man who's transformed into a giant insect.

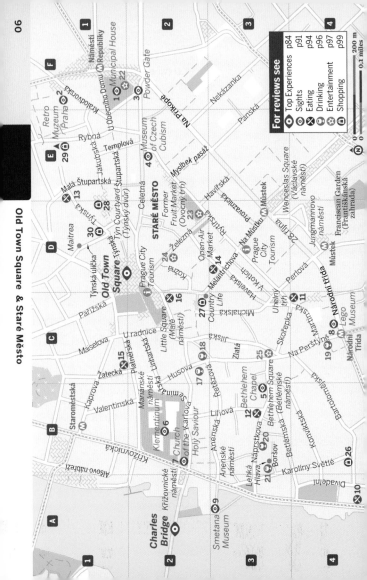

Old Town Square & Staré Město

For reviews see
- ◉ Top Experiences p84
- ⊙ Sights p91
- ⊗ Eating p94
- ⊙ Drinking p96
- ⊙ Entertainment p97
- ⊙ Shopping p99

0 ———— 200 m
0 ———— 0.1 miles

Sights

Municipal House HISTORIC BUILDING

1 ⊙ MAP P90, F1

Prague's most exuberantly art-nouveau building is a labour of love, with every detail of its design and decoration carefully considered, and every painting and sculpture loaded with symbolism. The **restaurant** (www.restauraceod.cz) and Kavárna Obecní Dům cafe (p97) here are like walk-in museums of art-nouveau design, while upstairs there are half a dozen sumptuously decorated halls that you can visit by guided tour. You can look around the lobby and the downstairs bar for free, or book a guided tour in the information centre.

The Municipal House stands on the site of the Royal Court, seat of Bohemia's kings from 1383 to 1483 (when Vladislav II moved to Prague Castle). The Royal Court was demolished at the end of the 19th century.

Between 1906 and 1912 this magnificent art-nouveau edifice was built in its place – a lavish joint effort by around 30 leading artists of the day, creating a cultural centre that was the architectural climax of the Czech National Revival. The mosaic above the entrance, **Homage to Prague**, is set between sculptures representing the oppression and rebirth of the Czech people. Other sculptures along the top of the facade represent history, literature, painting, music and architecture.

Municipal House

You pass beneath a wrought-iron and stained-glass canopy into an interior that is art nouveau down to the doorknobs. First stop on the guided tour is the Smetana Hall (p97), Prague's biggest concert hall, with seating for 1200. The stage is framed by sculptures representing the Vyšehrad legend (to the right) and Slavonic dances (to the left). On 28 October 1918 an independent Czechoslovak Republic was declared in the Smetana Hall, and in November 1989 meetings took place here between the Civic Forum and the Jakeš regime.

The Prague Spring (p76) music festival always opens on 12 May, the day the Czech composer Smetana died, with a procession from Vyšehrad to the Municipal House followed by a gala performance of his symphonic cycle *Má vlast* (My Country) in the Smetana Hall. Several impressive **official apartments** follow, but the highlight of the tour is the octagonal **Lord Mayor's Hall** (Primatorský sál), the windows of which overlook the main entrance. Every aspect of its decoration was designed by Alfons Mucha, who also painted the superbly moody murals that adorn the walls and ceiling.

Above you is an allegory of Slavic Concord, with intertwined figures representing the various Slavic peoples watched over by the Czech eagle. Figures from Czech history and mythology, representing the civic virtues, occupy the spaces between the eight arches. (www.obecnidum.cz)

Retro Muzeum Praha
MUSEUM

2 ◉ MAP P90, F1

A whiff of nostalgia hangs over this sprawling collection of household goods, clothing, appliances, toys and furnishings from the communist period. The styles on display will wow both budding historians and interior designers alike. The museum is situated on the 4th floor of the Kotva department store. There's lots of English signage to explain what everything means. (www.retromuzeumpraha.cz)

Powder Gate
TOWER

3 ◉ MAP P90, F2

Construction of the 65m-tall Powder Gate began in 1475 on the site of one of Staré Město's 13 original city gates. It remained unfinished until the great 19th-century neo-Gothicizer Jozef Mocker put the final touches to the building in 1886. The name comes from its use as a gunpowder magazine in the 18th century. The Gothic interior houses little more than a few information panels about the tower's construction – the main attraction is the view from the top. (www.prague.eu)

Museum of Czech Cubism
GALLERY

4 ◉ MAP P90, E2

Though dating from 1912, Josef Gočár's House of the Black Ma-

The Astronomical Clock's Spectacle

Every hour on the hour, crowds gather beneath the Old Town Hall Tower to watch the Astronomical Clock in action. It's an amusing – if slightly underwhelming – performance that takes just under a minute to finish. Most people simply stand and gawk, but it's worth understanding a bit of the clock's historic (and highly photogenic) symbolism.

The four figures beside the clock represent the deepest civic anxieties of 15th-century Praguers: Vanity (with a mirror), Greed (with his telltale money bag), Death (the skeleton) and Pagan Invasion (represented by a Turk). The four figures below these are the Chronicler, the Angel, he Astronomer and the Philosopher.

On the hour, Death rings a bell and inverts his hourglass, and the Twelve Apostles parade past the windows above the clock, nodding to the crowd. On the left side are Paul (with sword and book), Thomas (lance), Jude (book), Simon (saw), Bartholomew (book) and Barnabas (parchment); on the right side are Peter (with key), Matthew (axe), John (snake), Andrew (cross), Philip (cross) and James (mallet). At the end, a cock crows and the hour is rung.

donna (Dům U černé Matky Boží) – Prague's first and finest example of cubist architecture – still looks modern and dynamic. It houses an exhibition of the Museum of Decorative Arts' collection of cubist furniture, ceramics and glassware, as well as displays on Prague's unique cubist architecture and a cubist cafe. (www.czkubismus.cz)

Bethlehem Chapel   CHURCH

5 ◉ MAP P90, B3

The Bethlehem Chapel is a national cultural monument, being the birthplace of the Hussite cause. Jan Hus preached here from 1402 to 1412, marking the emergence of the Reform movement from the sanctuary of the Karolinum

(where he was rector). Every year on the night of 5 July, the eve of the anniversary of Hus's burning at the stake in 1415, a memorial is held here with speeches and bell-ringing. (www.bethlehemchapel.eu)

Klementinum   HISTORIC BUILDING

6 ◉ MAP P90, B2

The most overlooked of central Prague's attractions, the Klementinum is a vast complex of beautiful baroque and rococo halls, now mostly occupied by the **Czech National Library**. Most of the buildings are closed to the public, but you can walk through the courtyards, or take a 50-minute **guided tour** of the baroque Library Hall, the Meridian Hall, the Astronomical Tower and the Chapel of Mirrors. (www.klement inum.com)

Church of the Holy Saviour

CHURCH

7 ⊙ MAP P90, B2

When the Jesuits were invited to Prague by the Habsburg emperor, Ferdinand I, they selected one of the city's choicest pieces of real estate and in 1587 set to work on the Church of the Holy Saviour, Prague's flagship of the Counter-Reformation and the original church of the Klementinum (p93). The western facade faces Charles Bridge, its sooty stone saints glaring down at the traffic jam of trams and tourists on Křížovnické náměstí. Classical-music concerts are staged here (see www. pragueclassic.com for details). (www.farnostsalvator.cz)

Lego Museum

MUSEUM

8 ⊙ MAP P90, C4

This museum claims to have the largest private collection of Lego models in the world, with a play area at the end where kids can build stuff from Lego and a shop selling almost every set going. The exhibition doesn't quite justify the high admission price, however, unless you are a real Lego fanatic. (www.muzeumlega.cz)

Smetana Museum

MUSEUM

9 ⊙ MAP P90, A3

This small museum is devoted to Bedřich Smetana, Bohemia's favourite composer. It isn't that interesting, unless you're a Smetana fan, and has only limited labelling in English, but there's a good exhibit on popular culture's feverish response to Smetana's opera *The Bartered Bride* – it seems Smetana was the Andrew Lloyd Webber of his day. (www.nm.cz)

Eating

SmetanaQ Café & Bistro

BISTRO €

10 ✕ MAP P90, A4

SmetanaQ features a spacious interior with large windows overlooking the Vltava River and, in winter, a view of Prague Castle. Coffee (49Kč to 70Kč) comes from a local roaster, and the plentiful cakes, pies and breads are made in-house. Excellent breakfasts give way later in the day to more-ambitious, eclectic mains, like Asian pork belly and Slovak-style *halušky* (dumplings). (http://smetanaq. cz/#cafe-bistro)

U Dvou koček

CZECH €€

11 ✕ MAP P90, C4

A Prague classic, this traditional, been-here-forever beer hall and microbrewery, located under the arcading of Uhelný trh, is unmissable. The Urquell on tap is all well and good, but the restaurant's own Kočka lager better complements the hefty Bohemian fare on the menu.

Every Czech knows this restaurant from its starring role in one of the best-known 1980s Czech films, *Vrchní prchni!* (Waiter, Scarper!). (www.udvoukocek.cz)

V Zátiší

CZECH €€€

12 MAP P90, B3

For three decades, 'Still Life' has been one of Prague's top restaurants, and remains a great choice for a refined night out.

The decor is bold and modern, with huge pieces of quirky glassware, boldly patterned wallpapers and cappuccino-coloured crushed-velvet chairs. The menu ranges from high-end Indian cuisine to gourmet versions of traditional Czech dishes – the South Bohemian goose in plum sauce is superb. (www.vzatisi.cz)

Divinis

ITALIAN €€

13 MAP P90, E1

This restaurant has a playful decor in shades of cream enlivened with feature mirrors and splashes of cerise, and a homely clutter of shelves stacked with books, vases and odds and ends. Though Italian, the food is no pizza-pasta blowout, with the uncomplicated menu offering a choice of around eight starters and main courses. (www.divinis.cz)

Havelská Koruna

CAFETERIA €

14 MAP P90, D3

For a taste of old-school canteen fare that many Czechs eat daily, head to this self-service canteen north of Můstek. Pick up a *konzumační lístek* ('cosumption

Church of the Holy Saviour

Going Meatless in Old Town

Prague's oldest quarter is home to several good vegetarian and vegan spots. Our favourites:

Country Life (Map p90, C2; www.countrylife.cz) All-vegan cafeteria offering inexpensive salads, vegetarian goulash, sunflower-seed burgers and soy drinks.

Lehká Hlava (Map p90, B3; www.lehkahlava.cz) Down a narrow cul-de-sac, this simple, student-friendly spot exists in a little world of its own.

Maitrea (Map p90, D1; www.restaurace-maitrea.cz) Beautifully designed space with inventive vegetarian dishes.

chit') at the door, head to the serving counters where dinner ladies ladle out the staples of Bohemian and Moravian cuisine, eat at the communal benches and pay on the way out. (www.havelska-koruna.cz)

George Prime Steak STEAK €€€

15 MAP P90, C1

The 100% black Angus USDA Prime beef imported from the American Midwest is the name of the game here. Aged for at least 30 days, Prague's priciest cuts of meat are expertly braised and served with simple sides (just don't ask for your steak well done!). Pricey whiskies complete the menu at this sleek eatery. Dress in black and reserve.

U Prince INTERNATIONAL €€

16 MAP P90, C2

Guests are offered the standard array of Caesar and chef salads, plus burgers, grilled chicken breast and other ubiquitous mains.

Nevertheless, the focus here was never intended to be on the plate, but rather the awesome view over Old Town Square. Book your terrace seat well in advance. (www.hoteluprince.com)

Drinking

U Zlatého Tygra PUB

17 MAP P90, C2

Novelist Bohumil Hrabal's favourite tavern, the Golden Tiger is one of the few Old Town drinking holes that has hung on to its soul – and its reasonable prices (56Kč per 450mL of Pilsner Urquell). It's one of Prague's original pubs and is the place to which Václav Havel took Bill Clinton in 1994 to show him a real Czech pub. (www.uzlatehotygra.cz)

U Tří Růží BREWERY

18 MAP P90, C2

In the 19th century there were more than 20 breweries in Prague's Old Town, but by 1989 only one remained. The 'Three Roses' brewpub, on the site of one of those early breweries, helps revive the tradition, offering six beers on tap, including a tasty *světlý ležák* (pale lager), good food and convivial surroundings. (www.u3r.cz)

Kavárna Obecní Dům   CAFE

The spectacular cafe in Prague's opulent Municipal House (see 1 map p90, F1) offers the opportunity to sip your cappuccino amid an orgy of art-nouveau splendour. In addition to the original decor, the cafe is known for its outstanding, Vienna-style gateaus. (www.kavarnaod.cz)

U Medvídků   BEER HALL

19 MAP P90, C4

The most micro of Prague's microbreweries, with a capacity of only 250L, U Medvídků started producing its own beer in 2005, though its trad-style beer hall has been around for many years. The in-house restaurant serves good Czech food and there's a hotel upstairs. Dinner reservations are recommended. (www.umedvidku.cz)

Grand Cafe Orient   CAFE

There's food here, but most come to Prague's only cubist cafe in the Museum of Czech Cubism (see 4 map p90, E2) to sip a brew as an excuse to admire the unique styling, which includes everything from teaspoons to lampshades. The Orient was designed by Josef Gočár in 1912 and was restored and reopened in 2005, having been closed since 1920. Decent coffee and inexpensive cocktails, but occasionally surly service. (www.grandcafeorient.cz)

Café Kampus   CAFE

20 MAP P90, B3

This laid-back cafe doubles as an art gallery and event venue (talks, live music, lectures), and is popular with students from Charles University. There are Czech newspapers and books to leaf through, chilled tunes on the sound system, and a long menu of gourmet teas, coffees and spirits. (www.cafekampus.cz)

Hemingway Bar   COCKTAIL BAR

21 MAP P90, B3

The Hemingway is a snug and sophisticated hideaway with dark leather benches, a library-like back room, flickering candlelight, and polite and professional bartenders. There's a huge range of quality spirits (especially rum), first-class cocktails, champagne and cigars. Advance booking here is essential. (www.hemingwaybar.eu)

Entertainment

Smetana Hall   CLASSICAL MUSIC

22 MAP P90, F1

The Smetana Hall, centrepiece of the Municipal House (p91), is the city's largest classical concert hall, seating 1200 beneath an art-nouveau glass dome. The stage is framed by sculptures representing the Vyšehrad legend and Slavonic dances. It's the home venue of the Prague Symphony Orchestra (www.fok.cz), and stages music performances of all kinds. (www.obecnidum.cz)

Estates Theatre OPERA

23 ⭐ MAP P90, D2

The Estates is the oldest theatre in Prague, with performances taking place uninterrupted since 1783, and famed as the place where Mozart conducted the premiere of *Don Giovanni* on 29 October 1787. This, and other Mozart operas, are regularly performed here, along with a range of classic opera, ballet and drama. (www.narodni-divadlo.cz)

AghaRTA Jazz Centrum JAZZ

24 ⭐ MAP P90, D2

AghaRTA has been staging top-notch modern jazz, blues, funk and fusion since 1991, but moved into this central Old Town venue only in 2004. A typical jazz cellar with red-brick vaults, the centre also has a music shop (open 7pm to midnight) that sells CDs, T-shirts and coffee mugs. (www.agharta.cz)

Jazz Republic LIVE MUSIC

25 ⭐ MAP P90, C3

Despite the name, this relaxed club stages all kinds of live music, including rock, blues, reggae and fusion as well as jazz. Bands are mostly local, and the music is not overpowering – you can easily hold a conversation – which means it won't please the purists (sssshh!).

The Trials of Tycho Brahe

It's probably more than fair to describe Tycho Brahe, who's buried in the **Church of Our Lady Before Týn** (p85), as something of a character. This Danish father of modern astronomy catalogued thousands of stars, made stunningly accurate observations in an era before telescopes and helped his assistant Johannes Kepler derive the laws of planetary motion.

He came to Prague in 1599 as Emperor Rudolf II's official mathematician. But Brahe also dabbled in astrology and alchemy. He lost part of his nose in a duel and wore a metal replacement. As well as this his pet moose apparently drank too much beer, fell down the stairs and died.

In Prague, Brahe died in 1601 of a bladder infection, reputedly because he was too polite to go to the toilet during a long banquet. Only recently have historians decided he was probably poisoned instead. We're not sure which version is more comforting.

Admission is free. Books seats in advance. (www.jazzrepublic.cz)

Shopping

Kavka

BOOKS

26 🔒 MAP P90, B4

Arguably the best place in Prague to pick up books on Czech art and photography you simply won't find anywhere else. It stocks everything from large-format coffee-table books to small prints covering every genre and artist the country has produced. Also has an e-shop. (www.kavkaartbooks.com)

Modernista

HOMEWARES

Modernista specialises in reproduction 20th-century furniture, ceramics, glassware and jewellery in classic styles ranging from art deco and cubist to functionalist and Bauhaus. This branch, located in the Municipal House information centre (see 1 🗺 map p90, F1), is strong on jewellery and ceramics. (www.modernista.cz)

Manufaktura

ARTS & CRAFTS

27 🔒 MAP P90, C2

There are around a dozen of these kinds of Manufaktura outlets across town, but this small emporium near Old Town Square seems to keep its inventory especially enticing. You'll find great Czech wooden toys, beautiful-looking honey

gingerbread made from elaborate medieval moulds, and seasonal gifts such as hand-painted Easter eggs. (www.manufaktura.cz)

Botanicus

COSMETICS

28 🔒 MAP P90, D1

Around since the mid-90s, this now-international Czech chain produces natural health and beauty products made using herbs and plants grown on an organic farm in Ostrá, east of Prague. The scented soaps, herbal bath oils and shampoos, fruit cordials and handmade paper products make original souvenirs. (www.botanicus.cz)

Perníčkův sen

FOOD

29 🔒 MAP P90, E1

Sumptuous, fresh-baked gingerbread cookies and cakes to eat in or take home.

Bric A Brac

ANTIQUES

30 🔒 MAP P90, D1

This is a wonderfully cluttered cave of old household items, glassware, toys, apothecary jars, enamel signs, rusty bikes, typewriters and stringed instruments. Despite the junky look of the place, the knick-knacks (found in skips and attics across Bohemia) are shockingly expensive, but the affable Serbian owner can give you a guided tour around every piece in his extensive collection.

Explore
Wenceslas Square & Around

Busy Wenceslas Square, dating from 1348 and once a bustling horse market, was the site of several seminal events in Czech history. Today, it's crowded with souvenir shops, clubs, coffee chains and plenty of tourists, though it's possible to glimpse the square's previous grandeur simply by looking up at the glorious art-nouveau architecture.

The Short List

○ **Wenceslas Square (p102)** *The country's largest square is the capital's commercial centre and often the backdrop to political protest.*

○ **National Museum (p107)** *Fully renovated inside and out, this grand 19th-century museum is once again taking its rightful place as a top sight in Prague.*

○ **Mucha Museum (p107)** *An entire museum dedicated to the life and works of the most famous of Prague artists.*

○ **Hotel Jalta Nuclear Bunker (p109)** Hidden beneath the 1950s Hotel Jalta on Wenceslas Square lies a communist-era nuclear shelter that was opened to the public in 2013.

○ **Prague State Opera (p112)** *The recently renovated opera is one of Central Europe's best.*

Getting There & Around

Ⓜ Lines A and B cross at Můstek at the bottom of the square. Lines A and C meet at Muzeum at the top.

Neighbourhood Map on p106

Wenceslas Square (p102) ROMAN KYBUS/SHUTTERSTOCK ©

Top Experiences 📷
Stroll along
Buzzing Wenceslas Square

This massive central square was founded by Charles IV in 1348. For hundreds of years it was called the 'Horse Market' and featured horse-drawn trams and the first Czech theatre. On 28 October 1918, the independent republic of Czechoslovakia was announced here; in 1945 the end of WWII was declared and celebrated. Later, the square hosted huge, historic demonstrations.

⊙ MAP P108, C3

Václavské náměstí

🕐 24hr

Ⓜ Můstek, Muzeum

Jan Palach Memorial

In January 1969, university student Jan Palach set fire to himself in front of the National Museum to protest against the Soviet-led invasion of Czechoslovakia the preceding August. Palach later died from his wounds and became a national hero. The **memorial** sits at the exact spot where Palach fell, marked by a cross in the pavement just below the steps to the museum's entrance.

Former Radio Free Europe Building

During the Cold War, many Czechs and Slovaks turned to US-financed Radio Free Europe (RFE) for news from the West. After 1989 the radio moved its headquarters from Munich to the former Czechoslovak Federal Parliament building (just to the left of the National Museum). In 2008 RFE moved to a new building in the Prague suburbs, and the **old headquarters** (www.nm.cz) is now used as a National Museum annex.

St Wenceslas Statue

The focal point of Wenceslas Square is the equestrian statue of **St Wenceslas** at its southern end. Sculptor Josef Myslbek has surrounded the 10th-century Duke of Bohemia (and 'Good King Wenceslas' of Christmas-carol fame) with four other patron saints of Bohemia – Prokop, Adalbert, Agnes and Ludmila.

Grand Hotel Evropa

Grand indeed – this ornate **art-nouveau hotel** is easily the most colourful building on a colourful square. Unfortunately it was closed for renovation at the time of research.

★ Top Tips

o During holidays and festivals, try the square's food and drink stands for local specialities such as spiced wine and grilled sausage.

o Keep an eye on your belongings, especially at night – this area is notorious for pickpockets and touts.

o Many restaurants on the square are tourist traps; better-value options are nearby.

✕ Take a Break

Within the Lucerna shopping arcade on Wenceslas Square's southern side (enter from either Vodičkova or Štěpánská), the elegant, 1920s-style Kavárna Lucerna (p112) is a great place for a quick coffee.

Walking Tour 🥾

Tracing the Velvet Revolution

It's been well over three decades since 1989's Velvet Revolution, when Czechs peacefully overthrew their communist overlords, but it will always be a landmark event. This walk takes you past the sites of the large-scale protests, strikes and press conferences that heralded epic change in the country.

Start Národní třída;
Ⓜ Národní třída

Finish Former Radio Free Europe Building;
Ⓜ Muzeum

Length 1km; 45 minutes

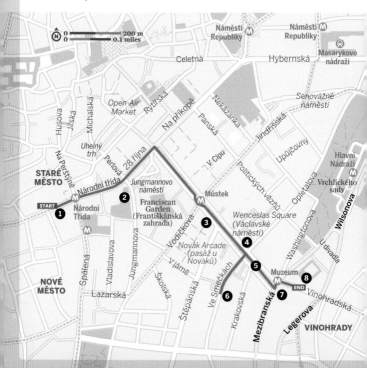

❶ Student Memorial

Start where the revolution itself began. The bronze **memorial** on the side of a lawyer's office marks the tragic events of 17 November 1989, when tens of thousands of students marching to remember Czechs murdered in WWII were attacked by riot police.

❷ Adria Palace

The beautiful, rondocubist **Adria Palace** (p111) temporarily served as the headquarters of Civic Forum, the umbrella group formed by Václav Havel to represent the protesters and their demands. In the weeks after 17 November, this was a beehive of dissident activity.

❸ Melantrich Building

The action soon spread to nearby Wenceslas Square and the **Melantrich Building**, now a Marks & Spencer. On 24 November, Havel and deposed 'Prague Spring' president Alexander Dubček addressed the crowds from its balcony.

❹ Hotel Jalta

Western journalists reported on the events from the balcony of the stern-looking **Hotel Jalta** (p109). A small museum in the hotel's basement shows off the sophisticated wiretapping set-up by the secret police to eavesdrop on hotel guests.

❺ St Wenceslas Statue

The **Wenceslas Statue** (p103), at the upper end of the square, was bedecked by protesters with flags, posters and political slogans.

❻ Činoherní Klub Theatre

Prague's theatres were used for public discussions. The Civic Forum was formed on 19 November at **Činoherní Klub Theatre** (Ve Smečkách 26) and immediately demanded the resignations of communist functionaries.

❼ Jan Palach Memorial

Just in front of the **National Museum** (p107) is the **Jan Palach Memorial** (p103), an inlaid cross for the student who set himself on fire in 1969 to protest the Soviet-led Warsaw Pact invasion of the previous year – becoming a national hero in the process.

❽ Former Radio Free Europe Building

At the top of the square, left of the National Museum, stands the former **Radio Free Europe Building** (p103), the US-funded radio station that helped bring down the communist regime. It now houses a branch of the National Museum.

Wenceslas Square & Around

For reviews see

◉	Top Experiences	p103
◉	Sights	p107
✕	Eating	p110
✕	Drinking	p111
✦	Entertainment	p112
⊞	Shopping	p113

Praha hlavní nádraží (Main Train Station)

Wilsonova

Vrchlického sady

Hlavní Nádraží Ⓜ

Senovážné náměstí

13 ●15

Jindřišská

Jeruzalémská

Upplova

Růžová

Opletalova

Washingtonova

Legerova

17 ✦

U divadla

Vinohradská

National Museum

1 ◉

Mezibranská

Senovážná

Nekázanka

Mucha Museum
2 ◉

Panská

Politických vězňů

Hotel Jalta
3 ● Nuclear Bunker

Muzeum Ⓜ

11 ✕

Krakovská

10 ✕

Ve Smečkách

Na Příkopě

20 ⊞

Havířská

V Jámě

Jindřišská

Můstek Ⓜ

22 ⊞

Lucerna Palace
4 ●
16 ✕ 18 ✦
19 ⊞ 12 ✕

Wenceslas Square ◉

Novák Arcade (pasáž u Nováků)

Štěpánská

Rytířská

Provaznická

Na Můstku

28 ⊞

Perlová

Uhelný trh

Jungmannovo náměstí

21 ⊞ Cubist Lamp Post
7 ⊞
6 ◉ Church of Our Lady of the Snows

8 ✕ 9 ✕

Franciscan Garden
5 ◉

Palackého

Vodičkova

Vlašská

Školská

14 ✕ Můstek

Národní Třída Ⓜ

Národní třída

Spálená

Purkyňova

Jungmannova

Vladislavova

Lazarská

Martinská

200 m
0.1 miles

Sights

National Museum

MUSEUM

1 ⊙ MAP P108, D4

Looming above Wenceslas Square is the neo-Renaissance bulk of the National Museum, designed in the 1880s by Josef Schulz as an architectural symbol of the Czech National Revival. Its magnificent interior is a shrine to the cultural development of the Czech lands. The permanent exhibitions focus on the 'miracle of evolution' and Czech history from the 8th to 20th centuries. (www.nm.cz)

Mucha Museum

GALLERY

2 ⊙ MAP P108, C1

This fascinating, busy museum features the sensuous art-nouveau posters, paintings and decorative panels of Alfons Mucha (1860–1939), as well as many sketches, photographs and other memorabilia. The exhibits include countless artworks showing Mucha's trademark Slavic maidens with flowing hair and piercing blue eyes, bearing symbolic garlands and linden boughs.

There are also photos of the artist's Paris studio, one of which shows a trouserless Gaugin playing the harmonium; a powerful canvas entitled *Old Woman in Winter;* and the original of the 1894 poster of actress Sarah Bernhardt as Giselda, which shot him to international fame.

In 1910 Mucha was invited to design the Lord Mayor's Hall in Prague's Municipal House (p91),

National Museum

Scenes of Oppression & Revolution

From Coup to Invasion

February 1948 marked the start of a half-century's worth of political turmoil in Prague. It was at this time that the leaders of the Communist Party of Czechlosovakia (KSČ), not content with a controlling position in the postwar coalition after the 1946 elections, staged a coup d'état backed by the Soviet Union. The next two decades saw widespread political persecution.

In the late 1960s, Communist Party leader Alexander Dubček loosened the reins slightly under the banner 'Socialism with a Human Face'. There was a resurgence in literature, theatre and film, led by the likes of Bohumil Hrabal, Václav Havel and Miloš Forman. The Soviet regime crushed this 'Prague Spring' on 20 and 21 August 1968, using Warsaw-Pact tanks, and Dubček was replaced by hard-liner Gustáv Husák.

The Fall of Communism

The Husák government expelled many pro-reform communists from positions of authority and introduced what Czechs called 'normalisation' – in other words, Soviet-style repression. Active dissent was limited to a few hundred people, mostly intellectuals and artists, including playwright Havel.

In November 1989, as communist regimes tumbled across Eastern Europe, the Czechoslovak government came under increasing pressure to relinquish power. On 17 November riot police cracked down on a peaceful student protest march, which would prove to be the catalyst to revolution.

Within days, crowds on Wenceslas Square swelled to some 500,000 people. A group led by Havel procured the government's resignation on 3 December, and 26 days later, he was the new leader. The 'Velvet Revolution', named for its peaceful nature (as well as the inspiration its leaders took from the rock band the Velvet Underground), had triumphed.

A Velvet Divorce

The transition to democracy was anything but smooth, though it eventually succeeded. One casualty of the revolution was the splitting of the country into separate Czech and Slovak states in 1993. The amicable break-up later became known as the 'Velvet Divorce'.

and following the creation of Czechoslovakia in 1918, he designed the new nation's banknotes and postage stamps.The museum's fascinating video documentary about Mucha's life is well worth watching, and helps put his achievements into perspective. (www.mucha.cz)

Hotel Jalta Nuclear Bunker   HISTORIC BUILDING

3 MAP P108, D3

Hidden beneath the 1950s Hotel Jalta on Wenceslas Square lies a communist-era nuclear shelter that was opened to the public in 2013. The tour, led by a guide in period security-police uniform, takes in a series of secret chambers. The highlight is the communications room, where wiretaps in the bedrooms of important guests were monitored. (http://en.muzeum-studene-valky.cz)

Koruna Palace   ARCHITECTURE

4 MAP P108, C3

An art-nouveau design by Antonín Pfeiffer, this shopping centre and office block has a tower topped with a crown of pearls. Note its charming facade around the corner from the Wenceslas Square entrance on Na příkopě. (www.koruna-palace.cz)

Franciscan Garden   PARK

5 MAP P108, B3

An unexpected, hidden oasis of peace and greenery lies just west of the bustle of Wenceslas Square. There are entrances from the end of the Světovor arcade off Vodičkova, the Alfa arcade off Wenceslas Square, and on Jungmannovo náměstí. It's a lovely place to enjoy a picnic on one of the many benches.

Church of Our Lady of the Snows   CHURCH

6 MAP P108, B2

This Gothic church at the northern end of Wenceslas Square was begun in the 14th century by Charles IV, but only the chancel was ever completed, which accounts for its proportions – seemingly taller than it is long.

Charles had intended it to be the largest church in Prague, but the Hussite wars brought work to an end. The nave is higher than that of St Vitus Cathedral, and the altar is the city's tallest. (www.pms.ofm.cz)

Cubist Lamp Post   PUBLIC ART

7 MAP P108, B2

Angular but slightly chunky, made from striated concrete – the world's only cubist lamp post is passed by many and overlooked by most.

It's a 1913 work by architect Emil Králíček, the man behind the Adamova Pharmacy on Wenceslas Square and Diamant House in Spálená St.

Eating

Styl & Interier

CAFE $$

8  MAP P108, C3

A passage opposite the Vodičkova entrance to the Lucerna Palace leads to this secret retreat, a rustic cafe with a high-walled garden, where local shoppers gather in wicker armchairs beneath the trees to enjoy coffee and cake, a lunch of quiche and salad or something heartier. Best to book a table. (www.stylainterier.cz/kavarna)

Cukrárna Myšák

CAFE $

9 MAP P108, C3

Opened by confectioner František Myšák in 1911 and redesigned by artist Josef Čapek (brother of Karel) in 1922, the Myšák has had a long and turbulent history, but has survived to this day as a classic Prague *cukrárna* (cafe bakery), albeit a pricey one in its current incarnation. Top-notch cakes, coffee and a super-central location make this a must-visit. (www.mysak.ambi.cz)

Výtopna

CZECH $$

10 MAP P108, D4

Got a soft spot for choo-choos, or kids who've had enough of Charles IV and Jan Hus? Then head for this gimmicky restaurant concept right on Wenceslas Square, where drinks can be delivered to guests' tables by model trains on long tracks. If you reserve online, make sure the staff know you want a table served by train. (www.vytopna.cz)

Výtopna

Much Ado about Mucha

Alfons Mucha (1860–1939) is the Czech answer to Austria's Gustav Klimt, England's William Morris or Scotland's Charles Rennie Mackintosh. One of the fathers – if not *the* father – of art nouveau as represented in the visual arts, he first found fame in Paris after producing a stunning poster for actress Sarah Bernhardt's 1895 play *Gismonda*. A contract with Bernhardt, reams of advertising work and trips to America brought him international renown.

Mucha returned home in 1909 and went on to design the banknotes for the first Czechoslovak Republic after 1918. Around this time, he also produced his opus, a collection of 20 gigantic canvases telling the history of the Slavic peoples, which he titled the *Slav Epic (Slovanská epopej)*. Mucha created some of the stunning interiors of Prague's **Municipal House** (p91) and designed a beautiful stained-glass window for **St Vitus Cathedral** (p42). His signature art-nouveau work is on display at the **Mucha Museum** (p107).

Mangal
TURKISH $$

11 MAP P108, D4

An unexpected sanctuary just a few paces from the brash bustle of Wenceslas Square, this family restaurant is 100% authentically Turkish, from the sizzling kebabs and meatballs to the crisp and savoury *pide* (Turkish 'pizza' filled with minced lamb and/or cheese). (www.mangalrestaurant.cz)

Dhaba Beas
VEGETARIAN $

12 MAP P108, C3

Dhaba Beas vegetarian self-service restaurants have been around in obscure parts of Prague for years, but this clean-cut version within the Lucerna passage is in an easily findable location and offers a stable selection of tasty salads, spicy mains and healthy drinks.

A bit of respite from pork knee, even for devoted carnivores. (www.dhababeas.cz)

Drinking

Vinograf
WINE BAR

13 MAP P108, E1

With knowledgeable staff, a relaxed atmosphere and an off-the-beaten-track feel, this appealingly modern wine bar is a great place to discover Moravian wines. There's also good finger food to accompany your wine. Very busy at weekends, when it's worth booking a table. (www.vinograf.cz)

Offstage
BAR

14 MAP P108, B2

The theatre bar of the Divadlo Bez zábradlí, located below the

Shopping
'At the Moat'

Crossing the lower (northern) end of Wenceslas Square, Na Příkopě is one of the city's prettiest and most popular promenades. The name translates as 'At the Moat' – the street traces a moat that once ran between Staré Město and Nové Město to protect the Old Town from attack.

In the 19th century, Na Příkopě was the fashionable haunt of Austrian cafe society. Today it's typical high-street shopping turf, lined with international retail chains such as H&M, Mango and Zara, and dotted with colourful shopping malls, including House of the Black Rose (dům U černé růže) at No 12, Myslbek pasáž (www.myslbek. com) at No 21, Slovanksý dům at No 22, and the Palladium (www.palladiumpraha.cz) at náměstí Republiky 1.

Adria Palace, is a relaxed, slightly upscale choice for a well-made cocktail, glass of wine or beer, and deep conversation. (www.offstagebar.cz)

Hoffa
COCKTAIL BAR

15   MAP P108, E1

Low-lit design is the key feature here with a long bar fronting a big wall of windows looking out onto Senovážné náměstí's fountain of dancing sprites. Friendly staff, accomplished cocktails and good food – you'll struggle to find a table at lunchtime. (www.hoffa.cz)

Kavárna Lucerna
CAFE

16   MAP P108, C3

The least touristy of Prague's grand cafes, the Lucerna is part of an art-nouveau shopping arcade designed by the grandfather of ex-president Václav Havel. Filled with faux marble, ornamental metal-work and glittering crystal lanterns (*lucerna* is Czech for lantern), this 1920s gem has arched windows overlooking Černý's famous sculpture, *Kůň*. (www.restaurace-monarchie.cz/en/cafe-lucerna)

Entertainment

Prague State Opera
OPERA

17   MAP P108, E3

The impressive neo-Renaissance State Opera was built in 1888 and originally served as the New German Theatre for the city's German-speaking community. It was lavishly renovated and reopened in 2020, and serves as Prague's pre-eminent venue for opera. (www.narodni-divadlo.cz)

Kino Světozor
CINEMA

18   MAP P108, C3

Movie buffs will want to check out this centrally located art-house cinema. Everything from the latest Czech films to classic movies and documentaries – often screened in the original language or with English subtitles (look for 'English-friendly' on the programme. (www.kinosvetozor.cz)

Lucerna Music Bar   LIVE MUSIC

19 MAP P108, C3

Nostalgia reigns supreme at this atmospheric old theatre, now looking a little dog-eared. It hosts all kinds of acts – from Czech superstars to amateur strummers from all over the country – plus there's a hugely popular 1980s and '90s video party from 9pm every Friday and Saturday night, with crowds of often not-so-young locals bopping along to Depeche Mode and Modern Talking. (www.musicbar.cz)

Shopping

Moser   GLASS

20 MAP P108, C1

The most exclusive and respected of Bohemian glass-makers, Moser was founded in Karlovy Vary in 1857 and is famous for its flamboyant designs. The shop on Na Příkopě is probably more for browsing than for the glass, as it's in a magnificently decorated, originally Gothic building called the House of the Black Rose (dům U černé růže). (www.moser-glass.com)

Baťa   SHOES

21 MAP P108, B2

Established by Tomáš Baťa in 1894, the Baťa footwear empire is still in family hands and is one of Czechia's most successful companies. The flagship store on Wenceslas Square, built in the 1920s, is considered a masterpiece of modern architecture and houses six floors of shoes, handbags, luggage and leather goods. (www.bata.cz)

Palác Knih Neo Luxor   BOOKS

22 MAP P108, C3

Palác Knih Neo Luxor is Prague's biggest bookshop – head inside to find a wide selection of fiction and nonfiction in English, German, French and Russian, including Czech authors in translation. (www.neoluxor.cz)

Explore ⬡
Nové Město

Nové Město is a long, arching, always busy neighbourhood that borders Staré Město on its eastern and southern edges. The name translates as 'New Town', which is something of a misnomer since the area was established nearly 700 years ago by Emperor Charles IV. But unlike Staré Město or Malá Strana, the historic feeling is missing here, owing mainly to massive reconstruction in the 19th century.

The Short List

○ **National Theatre (p121)** Built in the late 19th century with donations from around the Czech lands, this remains the country's top stage.

○ **Kavárna Slavia (p120)** The country's most famous cafe is a hangout for actors, writers and curious tourists.

○ **Náplavka Farmers Market (p123)** The capital's top outdoor market takes place by the sluggish waters of the Vltava.

○ **Reduta Jazz Club (p123)** Prague's premier jazz joint can compete with any in the world.

○ **U Fleků (p120)** The best-known of Prague's beer halls has been brewing beer for at least 500 years.

Getting There & Around
🚋 Take 2, 9, 18, 22, 23 to Národní třída.
Ⓜ Line B to Můstek or Karlovo Náměstí; Line A to Můstek.

Neighbourhood Map on p116

National Theatre (p121) STLJB/SHUTTERSTOCK ©

Nové Město

For reviews see

◉ Sights	p117
✕ Eating	p118
✕ ❍ Drinking	p120
☆ Entertainment	p121
🛍 Shopping	p123

200 m
0.1 miles

Muzeum Ⓜ

Wenceslas Square (Václavské náměstí)

Czech Blind United

Krakovská

Ve Smečkách

Mezibranská

Lucerna Palace (Palác Lucerna)

Štěpánská

Mústek Ⓜ

Na Rybníčku II

Ječná

Lipová

IP Pavlova

Franciscan Garden (Františkánská zahrada)

V Jámě

Školská

Navrátilova

Řeznická

Žitná

Palackého

Vodičkova

Jungmannova

Malá Štěpánská

Mústek Ⓜ

Adria Palace

K (David Černý Sculpture)

Vladislavova

Lazarská

Spálená

Charles Square (Karlovo náměstí)

Vyšehradská

Charles Square

Národní Třída Ⓜ

Národní Třída

Purkyňova

NOVÉ MĚSTO

Černá

Odborů

Spálená

Karlovo Náměstí

Na Pernštýně

Mikulandská

Václav Havel Library

Ostrovní

V Jirchářích

Voršilská

Opatovická

Křemencová

Myslíkova

Na Zderaze

National Memorial to the Heroes of the Heydrich Terror

Václavs

Bartolomějská

Národní třída

Pštrossová

Na Struze

Divadelní

Smetanovo nábřeží

Slav Island (Slovanský ostrov)

Masarykovo nábřeží

Vltava River

Vojtěšská

Šítkov

Jirásek Square (Jiráskovo náměstí)

Jirásek Bridge (Jiráskův most)

Dittrichov

Resslova

Václavs

Sights

Museum of Communism

MUSEUM

1 ⊙ MAP P104, E1

Put together by an American expat and his Czech partner, Prague's priciest private museum tells the story of Czechoslovakia's years behind the iron curtain in photos, words and a fascinating and varied collection. The empty shops, corruption, fear and doublespeak of life in socialist Czechoslovakia are well conveyed, and there are rare photos of the Stalin monument that once stood on Letná terrace. Be sure to watch the video about the protests leading up to the Velvet Revolution. (www.muzeum komunismu.cz)

Václav Havel Library

LIBRARY

2 ⊙ MAP P104, B2

This small exhibition and library, supported by the foundation that protects the legacy of the late playwright–president, houses a permanent exhibition on the life and work of Václav Havel, which includes fascinating photos from the ex-president's life. An English tour of the library can be arranged by emailing ahead. The archives are open for researchers every Tuesday from 9am until 5pm. (www.vaclavhavel-library.org)

Prague Main Train Station

ARCHITECTURE

3 ⊙ MAP P104, F2

What, a railway station as a tourist attraction? By no means all of it,

Museum of Communism

but it's certainly worth heading to the top floor for a look at the newly renovated splendour of the original art-nouveau entrance hall, designed by Josef Fanta and built between 1901 and 1909.

Museum of the Senses
SCIENCE CENTRE

4 ⊙ MAP P104, E1

A sure-fire winner with children, this interactive centre bamboozles visitors with its optical illusions. Have your head served on a platter of fruit, enter the infinity disco and the upside-down bathroom, or lie on a bed of nails. Also one of the best places in central Prague for children's birthday parties. (www. muzeumsmyslu.cz)

K (David Černý Sculpture)
PUBLIC ART

5 ⊙ MAP P104, C1

Located in the courtyard of the upmarket Quadrio shopping centre above Národní Třída metro station, David Černý's giant rotating bust of Franz Kafka is formed from 39 tonnes of mirrored stainless steel. It's a mesmerising show as Kafka's face rhythmically dissolves and re-emerges, possibly playing on notions of the author's everchanging personality and sense of self-doubt.

Charles Square
SQUARE

6 ⊙ MAP P104, C4

With an area of more than seven hectares, Charles Square is Prague's biggest – it's more like a small park, really, and was originally the city's cattle market. Presiding over it is the **Church of St Ignatius**, a 1660s baroque tour de force designed for the Jesuits by Carlo Lurago. The rather scruffy parkland has been slated for thorough gentrification for years.

Eating

Café Imperial
INTERNATIONAL €€

7 ✖ MAP P104, E1

First opened in 1914, and given a complete facelift in 2007, the Imperial is a tour de force of art-nouveau tiling – the walls and ceiling are covered in original ceramic tiles, mosaics, sculptured panels and bas-reliefs, with period light fittings and bronzes scattered about. The menu ranges from English breakfasts to Czech classics to roast quail. (www.cafeimperial.cz)

Globe Bookstore & Café
CAFE €

8 ✖ MAP P104, B3

This appealing expat bookshop-cafe serves nachos, burgers, chicken wings and salads until 11pm (to 10pm Sunday), and also offers an excellent brunch menu (9.30am to 3pm Saturday and Sunday) that includes an American classic (bacon, egg and hash browns), full English fry-up, blueberry pancakes and freshly squeezed juices. Lighter breakfasts are served from 10am to noon weekdays. (www. globebookstore.cz)

Heroic Paratroopers

In 1941, during WWII, the occupying Nazi government appointed SS General Reinhard Heydrich, Hitler's heir apparent, as Reichsprotektor of Bohemia and Moravia. The move came in response to a series of crippling strikes and sabotage operations by the Czech resistance movement, and Heydrich immediately cracked down on them with a vengeance.

In an effort to support the resistance and boost Czech morale, Britain secretly trained a team of Czechoslovak paratroopers to assassinate Heydrich. The daring mission was code-named 'Operation Anthropoid' – and against all odds, it succeeded. On 27 May 1942, two paratroopers, Jan Kubiš and Jozef Gabčík, attacked Heydrich as he rode in his official car through the city's Libeň district; he later died from his wounds.

The assassins and five co-conspirators fled but were betrayed in their hiding place in the Church of Sts Cyril & Methodius; all seven died in the ensuing siege. This moving story is told at the **National Memorial to the Heroes of the Heydrich Terror** (www.vhu.cz/muzea/ostatni-expozice/krypta), located at the church. The Nazis reacted with a frenzied wave of terror, which included the annihilation of two entire Czech villages, Ležáky and Lidice, and the shattering of the underground movement.

Klub Cestovatelů

MIDDLE EASTERN €€

9 MAP P104, A3

Run by travel enthusiasts, this Oriental-themed restaurant and tearoom cultivates a relaxed and welcoming atmosphere, with its wicker chairs, knick-knacks and library of travel guidebooks. The curries, falafel, hummus and kebabs have funny (and not-so-funny) names, such as the Butcher of Baghdad, Hungry Nomad and Sheik in the Hareem (it's a Czech thing!). It also hosts countless travel-related events that are not always in Czech. The cheap lunch menu (109Kč to 129Kč) is a steal. (www.klubcestovatelu.cz)

Art Restaurant Mánes

FRENCH €€

10 MAP P104, A3

Hidden around the back of the striking, functionalist, late-1920s facade of the **Mánes Gallery**, this gorgeous restaurant manages to be both welcoming and sophisticated, with its angular art-deco lines decorated with original ceiling frescoes by avant-garde Czech artist Emil Filla. The menu has an international flavour, but also lends a gourmet touch to a handful of Czech school-dinner classics. (www.manesrestaurant.cz)

Svatováclavská Cukrárna   CAFE €

11 ✕ MAP P104, C4

Join Czech grannies taking the cake at this oh-so-typical Czech *cukrárna* (cafe bakery), a little piece of the countryside in central Prague. The tables are tightly packed, the menu is a no-frills run-down of Bohemian pastries and cakes, and it all happens under the glass and brick arched roof of the mostly overlooked,overlooked art-deco Václavská arcade from the 1930s.

Knedlín   DUMPLINGS €

12 ✕ MAP P104, C1

Though for some inexplicable reason it's normally missing on restaurant menus, the filled dumpling is the ultimate Czech comfort food. This new, minimal-ist cafeteria takes the concept to the next level with inventive fillings such as mango and Thai spice featuring alongside the more usual school-canteen-style apricot and poppy seeds. Two make a cheap and filling meal. (www.knedlin.cz)

Drinking

Kavárna Slavia   CAFE

13 ☕ MAP P104, A1

The Slavia is the most famous of Prague's old cafes, a cherrywood-and-onyx shrine to art-deco

elegance, with polished limestone-topped tables and big windows overlooking the river. It has been a celebrated literary meeting place since the early 20th century – Rainer Maria Rilke and Franz Kafka hung out here, and it was frequented by Václav Havel and other dissidents in the 1970s and '80s. Best for a Turkish coffee and a slice of something nice on a rainy afternoon in the company of a good book. (www.cafeslavia.cz)

Cafe Louvre   CAFE

14 ☕ MAP P104, C1

The French-style Cafe Louvre is arguably the most amenable of Prague's grand cafes, as popular today as it was in the early 1900s when it was frequented by the likes of Franz Kafka and Albert Einstein. The atmosphere is wonderfully olde worlde, and it serves good Czech food as well as coffee. Check out the billiard hall and the ground-floor art gallery. (www.cafelouvre.cz)

U Fleků   BEER HALL

15 ☕ MAP P104, B3

A festive warren of drinking and dining rooms, U Fleků is a Prague institution, though it's usually clogged with tour groups high on oompah music and the tavern's home-brewed, slightly overpriced, 13-degree black beer (69Kč for 400mL). Purists grumble but go along anyway because the beer and atmosphere are good, though tourist prices have nudged out many locals. (www.ufleku.cz)

Kavárna Velryba CAFE

16 MAP P104, C2

The 'Whale' is a long-established, minimalist, arty cafe-bar – usually quiet enough to have a real conversation – with vegetarian-friendly snacks, a smoky back room and a basement art gallery. A clientele of Czech students, office workers and foreign backpackers. (www. kavarnavelryba.cz)

Pivovarský Dům Benedict BREWERY

17 MAP P104, D4

The old 'House of Beer' has undergone a bit of a rebranding since COVID-19, with a cleaned-up dining room – the dusty brewing paraphernalia has been carted off to a museum and the menu given an unfortunately bland international revamp. However, the wood-panelled pub itself is a pleasant place to linger, and the new Benedikt beer, brewed at Prague's Břevnov Monastery, provides relief from the Staropramen fizz. (www. pivo-dum.cz)

Entertainment

National Theatre THEATRE

18 MAP P104, A1

The much-loved National Theatre provides a stage for traditional opera, drama and ballet by the likes of Smetana, Shakespeare and Tchaikovsky (the *Nutcracker* is hopelessly sold out before Christmas), who share the programme alongside works by modern composers and playwrights. The box

Cafe Louvre

Literary Prague

The Czech Republic has a well-deserved reputation as a literary heavyweight. The names Franz Kafka and Milan Kundera will be familiar to any serious reader, but the country's (and city's) writing roots run deeper. It's no accident that the country's first postcommunist president, Václav Havel, was a playwright.

Czech Literary Lights

For many years, Prague was home to humourist Bohumil Hrabal (1914–97), whose many books are widely translated into English. The film based on his novel *Closely Watched Trains* won the Oscar for Best Foreign Film in 1968. Another near-household name is Jaroslav Hašek (1883–1923), whose book *The Good Soldier Švejk* is a stroke of comic genius that recalls something of *Catch-22*. Czech poet Jaroslav Seifert won the Nobel Prize in Literature in 1984.

The German Connection

In the 19th and early 20th centuries, Prague was a centre of German literature. Kafka (1883–1924), a German-speaking Jewish writer, remains the gold standard: his books *The Trial* and *The Castle*, among many others, are modern classics. But Prague was also home to Kafka's friend and publisher Max Brod (1883–1924), as well as noted writers Egon Erwin Kisch (1885–1948) and Franz Werfel (1890–1945). One of the most beloved poets in the German language, Rainer Maria Rilke (1875–1926), was born and studied in Prague.

New Voices

There's no shortage of new Czech literary talent: Jáchym Topol (b 1962), Petra Hůlová (b 1979), Michal Viewegh (b 1962), Sylvia Richterová (b 1945), Michal Ajvaz (b 1949) and Radka Denemarková (b 1968) have now taken their places among the country's leading authors. They are viewed as chroniclers of a very different, postcommunist age. Until recently, few books from these novelists had been translated into English. That's changing as publishers appear more willing to market them to English-speaking audiences.

offices are in the Nový síň building next door, in the Kolowrat Palace (opposite the Estates Theatre) and at the State Opera.

A performance here is a quintessentially Czech experience. Smart casual attire, at a minimum, is required. (www.narodni-divadlo.cz)

Reduta Jazz Club JAZZ

19 ⭐ MAP P104, C1

The Reduta is Prague's oldest jazz club, founded in 1958 during the communist era. It was here in 1994 that former US president Bill Clinton famously jammed on a new saxophone presented to him by Václav Havel. It has an intimate setting, with smartly dressed patrons squeezing into tiered seats and lounges to soak up the big-band and swing atmosphere. (www.redutajazzclub.cz)

Laterna Magika PERFORMING ARTS

20 ⭐ MAP P104, A1

Laterna Magika has been wowing audiences since its first cutting-edge multimedia show caused a stir at the 1958 Brussels World Fair. Its imaginative blend of dance, music and projected images continues to pull in the crowds. Nová Scena, the rather hideous glass cube next to the National Theatre, has been home to Laterna Magika since it moved here from its birthplace in the Adria Palace in the mid-1970s. (www.narodni-divadlo.cz)

Image Theatre PERFORMING ARTS

21 ⭐ MAP P104, C1

Established in 1989, this theatre company uses creative black-light theatre combined with pantomime, modern dance and video – not to mention liberal doses of slapstick – to tell its tales.

The staging can be very effective, but the atmosphere is often dictated by audience reaction. (www.imagetheatre.cz)

Wonderful Dvořák CLASSICAL MUSIC

22 ⭐ MAP P104, E4

The pretty little Vila Amerika was built in 1717 as an aristocrat's summer retreat. These days it's home to the **Dvořák Museum** (www.nm.cz) and from May to October, it stages performances of Dvořák's works by a chamber orchestra, complete with period costume. (www.musictheatre.cz)

Shopping

Náplavka Farmers' Market MARKET

23 🔒 MAP P104, A4

Stretching along the embankment from Trojická to Výtoň, this best-known of weekly markets makes the most of its riverside setting, with live music and outdoor tables scattered among stalls selling freshly baked bread, organic locally grown vegetables, homemade cakes and pastries, wild mushrooms (in season), herbs, flowers, wild honey, hot food, Czech cider, coffee and a range of arts and crafts.

The Náplavka is also the location of several barge bars in summer as well as arches fronted by the largest opening circular glass windows in the world. When there's nothing going on, the embankment returns to the swans and gulls that call the Vltava home, as well as the odd jogger. (www.farmarsketrziste.cz)

Walking Tour 🥾

Vyšehrad, Prague's Other Castle

The complex of buildings that make up the Vyšehrad Citadel has played an important role in Czech history for more than 1000 years. While few of the ancient buildings have survived, the citadel is still viewed as Prague's spiritual home. For more information and an events calendar, see www.praha-vysehrad.cz.

Start Tábor Gate;
Ⓜ Vyšehrad
Finish Cafe Citadela;
🚋 Výtoň
Length 1.5km; one hour

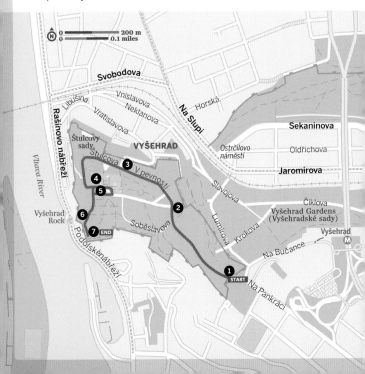

❶ Through the Old Gates

About 10 minutes on foot from the Vyšehrad metro station, heading west, you'll pass the **Tábor Gate** and the remains of the original Gothic **Špička Gate**.

❷ Prague's Oldest Building

The 11th-century Romanesque **Rotunda of St Martin** (www. praha-vysehrad.cz) is considered Prague's oldest surviving building. The structure has survived wars and gentrification and has been used as a prison, a poorhouse and a gunpowder store. It's only open during Mass (Monday and Wednesday at 6pm, Saturday at 8am).

❸ Into the Fortress

Through the **Brick Gate & Casements** (www.praha-vysehrad.cz) are hidden vaults used for imprisonment and weapon storage when Vyšehrad served as a fortress in the 18th century. The underground **Gorlice Hall** holds some of Charles Bridge's original statues.

❹ Dvořák's Final Resting Place

The 600 graves (many with intricately designed headstones) in the lovely gardens of **Vyšehrad Cemetery** (www.praha-vysehrad.cz) read like a who's who of Czech arts and letters, including musicians Antonín Dvořák and Bedřich Smetana, and artist Alfons Mucha.

❺ Last Church Standing

Dominating the southern Prague skyline, the neo-Gothic **Church of Sts Peter & Paul** (www.praha-vysehrad.cz) was one of Vyšehrad's few structures to avoid destruction in 1420 during the Hussite religious wars. The current facade dates from the 19th century and is the work of the great neo-Gothiciser, Josef Mocker.

❻ Underground History

The atmospheric **Gothic Cellar** (www.praha-vysehrad.cz) houses a worthwhile exhibit; its overview of the history of Prague's fortification helps put Vyšehrad's sights into perspective.

❼ Beer with a View

Along the southernb ramparts of the fortress', **Cafe Citadela** (www.facebook.com/cafecitadelavysehrad) is an outdoor beer garden with a relaxed vibe and nice views.

Explore ◈
Vinohrady & Žižkov

Vinohrady and Žižkov are the yin and yang of residential Prague. Gentrified Vinohrady boasts high-ceilinged, art-nouveau apartment buildings and is popular with young professionals and expats. The 'people's republic' of Žižkov is historically working class, rebellious and revolutionary, famed for its numerous pubs. Both are great to explore.

The Short List

○ **Café Kaaba (p135)** *This double act of neighbourhoods serves up some of the best nightlife in the capital in places like this cafe-bar.*

○ **Church of the Most Sacred Heart of Our Lord (p132)** *This 1930s work by a Slovene architect is possibly Prague's weirdest church.*

○ **National Monument (p131)** *Visit Hussite warlord Jan Žižka on his mighty steed before getting the lowdown on some Czechoslovak history.*

○ **TV Tower (p132)** *Prague's tallest structure has a restaurant at the top and babies crawling up and down its concrete length.*

○ **Riegrovy Sady (p132)** *Known for its beer garden, this large park is a relaxing place to escape the throngs.*

Getting There & Around

🚊 Line 4, 10, 13, 16 or 22 to Náměstí Míru, Lines 11 or 13 to Jiřiho z Poděbrad.

Ⓜ Line A to Náměstí Míru, Jiřiho z Poděbrad or Flora.

Neighbourhood Map on p130

National Monument (p131) SUN FREEZ/ALAMY STOCK PHOTO ©

Walking Tour 🚶

Pub & Wine Bar Tour of Vinohrady & Žižkov

In Prague, there's no better place to make a night of it: Žižkov, on one side, proudly claims to have more pubs per square metre than anywhere else on the planet; on the other side, classy Vinohrady is home to some serious wine and cocktail bars where the staff really know their mixology.

Start Vinohradský Parlament;
Ⓜ Náměstí Míru
Finish Bukowski's
🚋 Lipanská
Length 2.5km; one hour

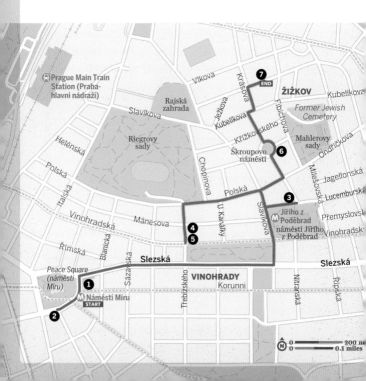

❶ Put Something in your Stomach

A sturdy meal is always a good idea if a night of drinking is on the cards. **Vinohradský Parlament** (p133), on Peace Square (náměstí Míru), offers excellent modern twists on Czech pub food, paired with the best beers the Staropramen brewery can muster.

❷ Night at the 'Museum'

Just across Peace Square, the **Prague Beer Museum** (www.praguebeermuseum.com) – actually a pub – offers around 30 regional Czech beers on tap, so once you've had your fill of Staropramen, see what else the country has to offer.

❸ French Wine with Style

One metro stop away, at Jiřího z Poděbrad, **Le Caveau** (www.broz-d.cz) offers the city's best selection of French wines and upmarket cheeses and snacks to match. Wine drinkers may want to start the night right here.

❹ Classy Cocktails at Bar & Books

At this stage, you can stay classy or go crazy. For classy, **Bar & Books Mánesova** (www.barandbooks.cz) is a sensuous cocktail lounge featuring lush, library-themed decor, top-shelf liquor and live music at weekends.

❺ Crazy Dancing at Termix

If crazy is the order of the night and it's after 10pm, gay-friendly **Termix** (p135) is the place to head. It stays open until 5am or so on weekends, so no need to move on if this is your scene.

❻ Beer at U Sadu

For more working-class libations, the congenial neighbourhood pub **U Sadu** (www.usadu.cz) is supremely popular with old locals, dreadlocked students and expats alike. Staff also run the kitchen past midnight, so if you're craving a snack, this may be your only option.

❼ Nightcap at Bukowski's

On the Žižkov street that's reckoned to have more drinking dens per metre than anywhere else in Prague, **Bukowski's** (www.facebook.com/bukowskisbar), named after the hard-drinking American poet Charles Bukowski, is a cut above its neighbours. Expect cool tunes and confident cocktails.

For reviews see

- ◉ Sights — p131
- ✖ Eating — p133
- ◓ Drinking — p135
- ✪ Entertainment — p135

Sights

National Monument   MUSEUM

1 ⊙ MAP P130, C2

While this monument's massive functionalist structure has all the elegance of a nuclear power station, the interior is a spectacular extravaganza of polished art-deco marble, gilt and mosaics, and is home to a fascinating museum of 20th-century Czechoslovak history. Although, strictly speaking, not a legacy of the communist era – it was completed in the 1930s – the huge monument atop Žižkov Hill is, in the minds of most Praguers over a certain age, inextricably linked with the Communist Party of Czechoslovakia. The monument's central hall houses a moving **war memorial** with sculptures by Jan Sturša. There are exhibits recording the founding of the Czechoslovak Republic in 1918, WWII, the 1948 coup, the Soviet invasion of 1968 and the Velvet Revolution of 1989.

Upstairs you can visit the Ceremonial Hall and the Presidential Lounge. But the most grimly fascinating part of the museum is the Frankenstein-like **laboratory** beneath the Liberation Hall, where scientists once battled to prevent communist leader Klement Gottwald's corpse from decomposing.

On display in a glass-walled sarcophagus by day, his body was lowered into this white-tiled crypt by night for another frantic round of maintenance and repair. (www. nm.cz)

National Monument

Riegrovy Sady GARDENS

2 ⊙ MAP P130, B4

Vinohrady's largest and prettiest park was designed as a classic English garden in the 19th century, and it's still a good place to put down a blanket and chill out. The back of the park affords photo-ops of Prague Castle.

Church of the Most Sacred Heart of Our Lord CHURCH

3 ⊙ MAP P130, D4

This church from 1932 is one of Prague's most original pieces of 20th-century architecture. It's the work of Jože Plečnik, a Slovene architect who also worked on 1920s additions to Prague Castle. The church is inspired by Egyptian temples and Christian basilicas.

It's open to the public during Mass but you might be able to sneak in at other times. (www.srdcepane.cz)

TV Tower TOWER

4 ⊙ MAP P130, D4

Prague's tallest landmark – and depending on your tastes, either its ugliest or its most futuristic feature – is the 216m-tall TV Tower, erected between 1985 and 1992. More bizarre than its architecture are the 10 giant crawling babies, which appear to be exploring the outside of the tower, by artist David Černý. (www.towerpark.cz)

New Jewish Cemetery CEMETERY

5 ⊙ MAP P130, D4

Franz Kafka is buried in this cemetery, which opened around 1890

Church of the Most Sacred Heart of Our Lord

How the Tower got its Babies

It was Czech artist-provacateur David Černý who first placed the creepy babies on the side of the Žižkov TV Tower in an installation called *Miminka* (Mummy), timed for Prague's reign as European Capital of Culture in 2000. The babies came down at the end of that year, but the resultant public outcry saw them reinstated, and it seems they're now a permanent fixture.

Art critics have differing views, but the babies *are* sporting slotted faces, like a USB drive, leading to one interpretation that the installation is intended as a commentary on our overdependence on media for sustenance. Or maybe not. Come to think of it, the tower *does* look a bit like a baby's bottle...

when the older Jewish cemetery – at the foot of the TV Tower – was closed. To find **Kafka's grave**, follow the main avenue east (signposted), turn right at row 21, then left at the wall; it's at the end of the 'block'. Fans make a pilgrimage on 3 June, the anniversary of his death. The entrance is beside Želivského metro station; men should cover their heads (yarmulkes are available at the gate). (www.kehilaprag.cz)

Eating

Benjamin INTERNATIONAL €€€

6 🍴 MAP P130, D6

Vršovice may be low on cool restaurants, but it does have one of Prague's most prized fine-dining establishments. Benjamin serves just 10 guests a night at its horseshoe-shaped counter. The choice is a five- or eight-course menu, featuring fancy dishes inspired by old Czech recipes. Reservations required. (www.benjamin14.cz)

Kofein SPANISH €€

7 🍴 MAP P130, C5

Tapas is nothing new in the Czech capital but few do it as well as this family-run restaurant near náměstí Jiřího z Poděbrad. You will search in vain for many Czech staples among the tiger prawns, grilled octopus, Ibérico ham and Raclette cheese, but the wine list is surprisingly patriotic, with even Bohemian red from Mělník appearing on the card. Book ahead. (www.ikofein.cz)

Vinohradský Parlament CZECH €€

8 🍴 MAP P130, A5

This clean, bright pub features a handsome, early-modern, art-nouveau interior and a daring, inventive cooking staff who are willing to look beyond the standard pork and duck to other traditional

Brussels in Prague

Design buffs beware. When Czechs talk about 'Brussels style', they're not referring to Belgian art nouveau or anything related to Henry Van de Velde. Rather, they're harking back to a heyday of their own national design when, despite the constraints of working under a communist regime, Czechoslovakia triumphed with its circular restaurant pavilion at the 1958 Brussels Expo. More than 100 local designers took away awards, including porcelain designer Jaroslav Ježek, who won the Grand Prix for his Elka coffee service. The aesthetics of the time were similar to what you see at **Café Kaaba** (p135). For a more authentic take, visit **Veletržní Palác** (p138).

Czech staples such as goose, rabbit, and boar. Phone ahead to book as it's often packed. (www.vinohrad skyparlament.cz)

Hostinec U Tunelu   CZECH €

9 ⊗ MAP P130, D1

At the mouth of the pedestrian tunnel linking Žižkov with Karlín, this weekday-only, retro-styled 1920s tavern serves a cheap mix of local and mildly exotic lunch specials until 2pm, after which it reverts to Czech beer snacks such as fried cheese, pickled sausages and beef with horseradish. The simple woody dining room is perfect for sipping a Konrad or Kocour beer. (www.utunelu.cz)

Pastička   CZECH €€

10 ⊗ MAP P130, B4

A warm, inviting ground-floor pub with a little garden out the back, Pastička is great for a beer or a meal. The interior design is part 1920s Prague and part Irish pub.

Most come for the Urquell, but the mix of international and traditional Czech dishes is also worth a visit. (www.restaurace-pasticka.cz)

The Tavern   BURGERS €

11 ⊗ MAP P130, B3

This cosy sit-down burger joint is the dream of a husband-and-wife team of American expats who wanted to create the perfect burger using organic products. Great pulled-pork sandwiches and different kinds of veggie burgers, too. Reserve online. (www.thetavern.cz)

U Bulínů   CZECH €€

12 ⊗ MAP P130, B5

Delicious traditional Czech cooking served in an old-fashioned, warm setting. Try goulash with potato pancakes, *strapačky* (small flour and potato dumplings served with sheep's cheese) and other local specialities. The lunch specials are good value and there's a small terrace. (www.restauraceubulinu.cz)

Drinking

Café Kaaba

CAFE

13 MAP P130, A4

Café Kaaba is a stylish little cafe-bar with retro furniture and pastel-coloured decor that comes straight out of the 1959 Ideal Homes Exhibition. It serves up excellent coffee made with freshly ground imported beans.

U Slovanské Lípy

PUB

14 MAP P130, D2

Žižkov's oldest pub, but plain and unassuming in and out, 'At the Linden Tree' (the linden is a Czech national emblem) is something of a place of pilgrimage for local lager lovers. The reason is its range of rare artisan brews from all over the country, anything from Krušnohor from the remote northwest to Albrecht from distant Frýdlant. (www.uslovanskelipy.cz)

Planeta Žižkov

PUB

15 MAP P130, D2

The legendary Planet is a wonderful Žižkov boozer serving dewy tankards of Urquell and Kozel as well as elephantine portions of Czech pub-resto food such as fried cheese, pork knuckle and goulash with dumplings. The eclectic interior runs from Viktoria Žižkov football scarves to jumble-sale furniture, and the clientele is mostly Žižkováci (natives of the planet). (www.planetazizkov.cz)

Entertainment

Palác Akropolis

LIVE MUSIC

16 MAP P130, C3

The Akropolis is a Prague institution, a labyrinthine, sticky-floored shrine to alt music and drama. Its various performance spaces host a smorgasbord of musical events, from DJs and string quartets to Macedonian Roma bands, local punk gods and visiting talent – Marianne Faithfull, The Flaming Lips and The Strokes have all played here. (www.palacakropolis.cz)

Techtle Mechtle

CLUB

17 MAP P130, B4

This cellar dance-bar came to national attention during the pandemic, but let's not talk about that. The name translates to 'Hanky Panky' in Czech, and that's what most of the Czech Q-list celebs who come here are after (not respiratory ailments). In addition to a cocktail bar, you'll find a decent restaurant and dance floor. Arrive early. (www.techtle-mechtle.cz)

Termix

CLUB

18 MAP P130, B4

Termix is one of Prague's most popular gay dance clubs, with an industrial, tech vibe (lots of shiny steel, glass and plush sofas) and a young crowd that includes as many tourists as locals. The smallish dance floor fills up fast, and you may have to queue to get in. (www.club-termix.cz)

Explore

Holešovice

In Holešovice, you start to appreciate Prague as a genuine working city. Though sections of this former industrial quarter remain run-down (particularly in the eastern part of the neighbourhood), the area has been slowly gentrifying and is slated one day to become Prague's 'Art District'. The hilltop beer garden at Letná is a relaxing spot on a warm summer evening, while the National Gallery's impressive holdings at Veletržní Palác may make for Prague's most underrated museum.

The Short List

○ **Veletržní Palác (p138)** *Top billing in the neighbourhood goes to the National Gallery's modern- and contemporary-art exhibition.*

○ **Prague Zoo (p142)** *The best zoo in the country can be found on a steep hill on the north bank of the River Vltava.*

○ **National Technical Museum (p141)** *One of the best places in the capital to take the children, especially on a rainy day.*

○ **Letná Gardens (p141)** *Overlooking the old centre, this park is a great place to grab a beer or unfurl a picnic blanket.*

○ **The Eatery (p142)** *Holešovice is the latest Prague suburb to be awarded the title 'up-and-coming', thanks to its cool eating and nightlife at places like this one.*

Getting There & Around

🚋 Lines 1, 8, 12, 25, 26 to Letenské náměstí; Lines 1, 6, 8, 12, 25, 26 to Strossmayerovo náměstí.

Ⓜ Line C to Vltavská or Nádraží Holešovice.

Neighbourhood Map on p140

Strossmayerovo Square, Holešovice SHARKSHOCK/SHUTTERSTOCK ©

Top Experience 📷

Get your Art Fix at Veletržní Palác

The National Gallery's collection of art from the 19th, 20th and 21st centuries is a must for art lovers, particularly fans of impressionism, constructivism, cubism and surrealism. The holdings are strong on French impressionists, early modern masters such as Schiele, Klimt and Picasso, and the generation of Czech artists working in the 1920s and '30s.

◎ MAP P130

Trade Fair Palace

www.ngprague.cz

Dukelských hrdinů 47

🚊 1, 6, 8, 12, 14, 17, 25, 26
Ⓜ Vltavská,

French Collection

Thanks to an enduring Bohemian interest in French painting, the palace's 3rd floor has an impressive collection of late-19th- and 20th-century French art. Artists represented at the palace include Monet, Gauguin, Cézanne, Picasso, Delacroix and Rodin. Look for Gauguin's *Flight* and Van Gogh's *Green Wheat*.

Avant-Garde Czech Art

The museum's display of interwar (1918–38) Czech art (also on the 3rd floor) is one of the country's finest. Standouts include the geometric works by František Kupka, and cubist paintings, ceramics and design by several different artists – these paintings show an interesting parallel with the concurrent art scene in Paris.

The 'Long' Century

The palace's 4th floor shows off the breathtaking landscapes and portraiture of the 19th century (which the curators define here as from 1796–1918). The exhibition boasts works by some major names: Klimt, Schiele and Munch, to name a few. Two highlights take on feminine themes: Klimt's luscious, vibrantly hued *The Virgins* and Schiele's much darker, foreboding *Pregnant Woman and Death*.

Prague's National Gallery

The Veletržní Palác (Trade Fair Palace) is just one branch of the National Gallery. For 500Kč, you can buy a ticket for combined admission to all of the National Gallery's buildings that host permanent exhibitions, including Schwarzenberg Palace, Šternberg Palace (p49) and the Convent of St Agnes (p75), as well as the Trade Fair Palace.

★ **Top Tips**

o The museum is huge. If you only have an hour or two, just hit the highlights listed here.

o Children and young adults up to 26 years of age enjoy free admission.

o Pick up Prague postcards or souvenirs at the museum shop.

✕ **Take a Break**

The museum cafe, located on the ground floor and open during museum hours, is convenient for a coffee.

Just across the road is **U Houbaře** (www.u-houbare.cz), an old-school pub with a cheap menu.

Holešovice Get your Art Fix at Veletržní Palác

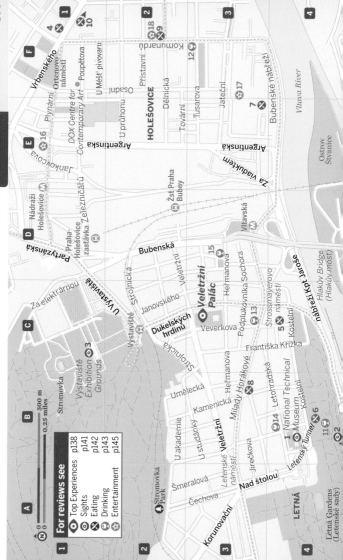

For reviews see

Top Experiences	p138
Sights	p141
Eating	p142
Drinking	p143
Entertainment	p145

0 — 500 m
0 — 0.25 miles

Stromovka

Vystaviště Exhibition Grounds 3

Za elektrárnou

U Výstaviště

Vystaviště

Strojnická

Janovského

Dukelských hrdinů

Strojnická

Veverkova

Veletržní Palác

13

5 Kostelní

Podplukovníka Sochora

Strossmayerovo náměstí

nábřeží Kpt Jaroše

Hlávkův Bridge (Hlávkův most)

Hermanova

15

Bubenská

Veletržní

Janovského

Umělecká

Kamenická

Milady Horákové

Letohradská

Hermanova

Frantíška Křížka

8

14

National Technical Museum 6

11

2

Letenský Tunnel

Kostelní

LETNÁ

Letná Gardens (Letenské sady)

U akademie

U studánky

Veletržní náměstí

Letenské náměstí

Jirečkova

Nad štolou

Korunovační

Čechova

Šmeralová

Stromovka Park

Partyzánská

Nádraží Holešovice

Jankovcova

16

E

Plynární

Ortenovo náměstí

Vrbenského

4

1

10

18 9

2

Komunardů

DOX Centre for Contemporary Art • Poupětova

U Měšť pivovaru

Jupeso

U průhonu

Osadní

Přístavní

12

HOLEŠOVICE

Dělnická

Tovární

Tusarova

Jateční

17

7

Bubenské nábřeží

Argentinská

Za Viaduktem

Argentinská

Praha-Holešovice zastávka Železničářů

Žst Praha Bubny

Bubenská

Veletržní

Vltavská

Vltava River

Ostrov Štvanice

Partyzánská

Sights

National Technical Museum

MUSEUM

1 ⊙ MAP P106, B4

Prague's family-friendly National Technical Museum is a dazzling presentation of the country's industrial heritage. The exhibits here are anything but dull. Start in the main hall, filled to the rafters with historic planes, trains and automobiles then continue on to astronomy, photography, printing and architecture. (www.ntm.cz)

Letná Gardens

PARK

2 ⊙ MAP P106, B4

Lovely Letná Gardens occupies a bluff over the Vltava River, north of the Old Town, and has postcard-perfect views out over the city, river and bridges. It's ideal for walking, jogging and drinking at the popular Letná Beer Garden (p143) at the eastern end of the park. From the Old Town, find the entrance up a steep staircase at the northern end of Pařížská ulice (across the bridge). Alternatively, take the tram to Letenské náměstí and walk south for 10 minutes.

Výstaviště Exhibition Grounds

CULTURAL CENTRE

3 ⊙ MAP P106, C1

This sprawling, somewhat neglected area of attractions and buildings was first laid out for the 1891 Jubilee Exhibition. It holds mainly trade fairs (see the website

National Technical Museum

GEORGIOS TSICHLIS/SHUTTERSTOCK ©

Prague Zoo

Prague's attractive **zoo** (Map p106; www.zoopraha.cz) is set on 60 hectares of wooded grounds on the banks of the Vltava. It makes for a great outing for kids. There are sizeable collections of giraffes and gorillas, but pride of place goes to a herd of rare horses. Attractions include a miniature cable car and a big play area.

for a calendar) and open-air rock concerts, but also has a branch of the National Museum. It's an easy walk from here to Stromovka Park (p145). (www.incheba.cz)

Eating

The Eatery
CZECH €€

4 MAP P106, F1

The Eatery is the best restaurant in eastern Holešovice, hands-down. The sophisticated space, bathed in steel and tones of grey, shuttles out local, seasonal dishes from an open kitchen. Think Czech food, but with a modern twist – braised beef with potato purée and bone-marrow crumble, or pheasant. The wine menu is delightfully long. (www.theeatery.cz)

Bistro 8
INTERNATIONAL €

5 MAP P106, C4

This tiny cafe-bistro solidifies this street's claim to being the coolest spot in Holešovice. The menu consists mainly of fresh-made soups and sandwiches, plus a tempting array of cakes and excellent coffees. There are a few tables inside

and some pavement spots to sit in nice weather. (www.bistro8.cz)

Letenský Zámeček
CZECH €€

6 MAP P106, B4

This upscale brasserie occupies the ground floor of a 19th-century chateau next to the Letná Beer Garden (p143). It's open year-round but comes into its own from May to September, with the outdoor terrace open and the spires of the Old Town stretching out in the distance. The kitchen is strong on Czech specialities such as duck breast with red cabbage purée, and wild boar. (www.letenskyzamecek.cz)

Tràng An Restaurace
VIETNAMESE €

7 MAP P106, E3

Holešovice's **Prague Market** (www. prazska-trznice.cz) is slowly renovating but still looks run down. This family-run Vietnamese restaurant is a solid reason to visit. Queue at the counter and choose from a large picture menu on the wall. There's plenty of indoor seating and outside picnic tables in nice weather. Try to visit before or after typical meal times to avoid a wait. (www.facebook.com/asijskebistro podosmickou)

Mr Hot Dog
AMERICAN €

8 🍴 MAP P106, B3

This fast-food restaurant is a cult favourite for its gourmet hot dogs, but the sliders (mini hamburgers) and cheese fries hit the spot, too. Chow down while head-bopping to hip-hop, or order takeaway. The location is handy for dropping in before or after an afternoon at the nearby Letná Beer Garden (p143). (www.mrhotdog.cz)

Phill's Corner
INTERNATIONAL €

9 🍴 MAP P106, F2

This bright, modern corner restaurant draws design inspiration from Holešovice's industrial past and its culinary cues from kitchens around the world, including flavours from Asia and the Middle East. The daily lunch menu of soup and a main course for around 150Kč is a great deal. (www. phillscorner.cz)

Pivovar Marina
ITALIAN €€€

10 🍴 MAP P106, F1

An unlikely but welcome combination: an excellent Czech microbrewery and proper Italian cooking. For beers, the wheat beer and 10-degree Přístavní lager are certainly worth trying. The food includes high-end pasta and mains such as Wagyu steak. During the warmer months, the outdoor tables afford relaxing views over the river. (www.pivovarmarina.cz)

Drinking

Letná Beer Garden
BEER GARDEN

11 🍺 MAP P106, B4

No accounting of watering holes in Holešovice would be complete without a nod towards the city's best beer garden, with an amazing panorama, situated at the eastern end of the Letná Gardens (p141). Buy a takeaway beer from a small kiosk and grab a picnic table. Kiosks also sell small food items such as chips and sandwiches. (www.letenskyzamecek.cz)

Holešovice Drinking

DOX Centre for Contemporary Art

Just a short tram ride from Veletržní Palác, the **DOX Centre for Contemporary Art** (Map p106, F1; www.dox.cz) is a private gallery and museum that's trying to re-establish Holešovice's reputation as the repository of Prague's best modern art. The minimalist multilevel building occupies an entire corner block, providing Prague's most capacious gallery space, studded with a diverse range of thought-provoking contemporary art and photography. Don't miss DOX's excellent cafe and bookshop.

Vnitroblock

CAFE

12 MAP P106, F3

Hidden in the back of an industrial building, Vnitroblock is the coolest daytime hangout in Holešovice. There's a pop-up kitchen, sneaker store and cafe, but contemporary art on the exposed brick walls makes it an art gallery, too. Dogs lounge beneath tables while their owners work on laptops. (www.vnitroblock.cz)

Cobra

BAR

13 MAP P106, C3

This all-purpose cafe, dinner spot and late-night bar has something for everyone: very good coffee and tea, microbrews and well-made cocktails. There's also an open kitchen at the back that serves up a weekly soup and main-course meal choices. The menu is filled with vegan options. (www.barcobra.cz)

Café Letka

CAFE

14 MAP P106, B4

Family-, pet- and laptop-friendly Café Letka is a rustic space with large windows. Sit at a large central table or by the window and order coffee made with beans from Berlin roaster Five Elephants. It's located behind the National Technical Museum (p141) and shares an entrance with the children's theatre Pidivadlo. (www.cafeletka.cz)

Kavárna Liberál

CAFE

15 MAP P106, D3

This Viennese-style coffee house captures something of Prague in

Cross Club

Stromovka Park

Prague's largest central park, **Stromovka** (Map p106, A2), has gotten a major facelift in the past couple of years and now arguably ranks as the city's prettiest park. Stromovka was once a medieval hunting ground for royals; now it's popular with strollers, joggers, cyclists and inline skaters. Kids can climb on the huge gnarled branches of ancient fallen trees, or play at one of several playgrounds – and adults will appreciate the exquisite landscaping and lavish displays of flowers.

the 1920s. By day, it's a quiet spot for coffee and connecting with wi-fi; evenings bring out a more pub-like feel. There are occasional live bands in the basement. The menu includes coffee, beer and wine and light foods such as salads and omelettes. Often it will have excellent sweets such as cheesecake and apple strudel. (www.facebook.com/kavarnaliberal)

Entertainment

Cross Club CLUB

 16 MAP P106, E1

An industrial club in every sense: the setting in an industrial zone, the thumping music (both DJs and live acts), and the structure – a must-see maze of gadgets, shafts, cranks and pipes, many of which move and pulsate with light to the music. The programme includes occasional live music, theatre performances and art happenings. It also has a cafe, open 2pm to 2am. (www.crossclub.cz)

Jatka 78 ARTS CENTER

 17 MAP P106, F3

This alternative art space, housed in a former slaughterhouse in Holešovice's Prague Market (p142), stages performances from dance to circus and acrobatics. Many shows are kid-friendly. It's worth grabbing a bite at the bistro before or after – the meals, including sandwiches and pasta, are reasonably priced, and there's a family play area, too. (www.jatka78.cz)

La Fabrika PERFORMING ARTS

 18 MAP P106, F2

The name refers to a 'factory', but this is actually a former paint warehouse that's been converted into an experimental performance space. Depending on the night, there's live music (jazz or cabaret), theatre, dance or film. Consult the website for the latest programme. Try to reserve in advance as shows typically sell out. (www.lafabrika.cz)

Survival Guide

Before You Go

Book Your Stay

o Consider splurging for air-conditioning from mid-June through August.

o Parking can be tight. If driving, work out parking details with the hotel in advance and avoid hotels in Malá Strana and the Old Town.

o Many private singles or doubles in hostels are very nice and offer excellent value.

o You can often find last-minute bargains for top-end hotels on the standard online booking sites.

o Malá Strana is a particularly scenic location in which to stay, but it's worth considering a room in one of Prague's suburbs such as Vinohrady, Smíchov or Holešovice, as central Prague is easily reached by public transport.

Useful Websites

Most Prague hotels and short-term apart-

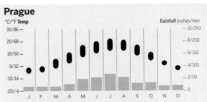

Prague
°C/°F Temp   Rainfall inches/mm

When to Go

o **Spring (Apr–Jun)**
April is the start of the tourist season. Accommodation books up at Easter and for the Prague Spring music festival in May.

o **Summer (Jul–Aug)**
Sunny and occasionally hot. All attractions open.

o **Autumn (Sep–Oct)**
Often sunny but cool. A handful of attractions close on 1 October for winter.

o **Winter (Nov–Mar)**
Short, dark days and occasionally snow. Tourists descend for lively Christmas and New Year festivities.

ment rentals are listed on well-known booking websites like **Booking. com** (www.booking. com) or **Airbnb** (www. airbnb.com). Locally owned room-finding services can occasionally offer better value and locations.

Prague City Apartments (www.prague-city-apartments.cz) Offers short- and long-term accommodation in one- and two-person studios and larger apartments at good locations around the Old Town.

Apartments Praha 6 (https://apartments-

prague6.com) Family-run outfit in outlying Břevnov maintains around 15 apartments in quiet suburban locations, well away from the summer-time crowds in the centre of town.

Lonely Planet (www. lonelyplanet.com) Author-recommended reviews.

Best Budget

o **Sir Toby's Hostel** (www.sirtobys.com) Dorms in a refurbished apartment building with a spacious kitchen and common room.

Sophie's Hostel
(www.sophieshostel.
com) Hostel for a gentler
sort of budget traveller,
with a touch of contem-
porary style.

Ahoy! Hostel (www.
ahoyhostel.com)
Welcoming and peaceful
hostel with eager-to-
please staff and 'arty'
decoration.

Prague Central Camp
(www.praguecentral
camp.com) Prague's
most central campsite,
located in Žižkov.

ArtHarmony (www.
artharmony.cz) Central
guesthouse with gim-
micky decor.

Best
Midrange

Romantik Hotel
U Raka (www.hotelu
raka.cz) Blissful rural-
style hotel in the tranquil
Nový Svět neighbour-
hood.

Mama Shelter
Prague (www.
mamashelter.com)
Quirky design hotel in
Holešovice.

Icon Hotel (www.icon
hotel.eu) A very trendy
designer hotel sporting
lots of 21st-century
conveniences.

Hunger Wall
Residence (www.
hungerwall-residence.
com) Spotlessly clean
and modernised short-
stay apartments.

Dům U Velké Boty
(www.dumuvelkeboty.
cz) Old pension set on a
quiet square.

Best
Top End

Golden Well Hotel
(www.goldenwell.cz)
Historic, luxury hotel in
the ultimate location –
beneath the castle walls.

Aria (www.ariahotel.
net) Five-star luxury with
a musical theme.

Dominican Hotel
(www.axxoshotels.com/
the-dominican) Housed
in a former monastery
and bursting with
character.

Alcron Hotel (www.
alcronhotel.com)
Central, five-star hotel
with a Michelin-starred
restaurant.

Le Palais Hotel
(www.lepalaishotel.eu)
Luxury hotel housed in a
gorgeous belle-époque
building.

Arriving in Prague

Václav Havel Airport Prague

This international
airport (www.prg.aero) is
17km west of the city
centre.

Airport Express (AE)
Bus Runs between the
airport and Prague's main
train station at 30-minute
intervals. Service starts
at 5am and the last bus
leaves around 9.30pm.
Buy tickets (adult/conces-
sion 100/50Kč) from
the driver.

Taxi.eu (https://taxi-
airport-prague.com)
The official airport taxi
company. Taxis line up
outside the Arrivals halls
of both terminals. A ride
to náměstí Republiky in
the centre costs about
700Kč.

Bus 119 This city
bus terminates at the
closest metro station
to the airport, Nádraží
Veleslavín (Line A). The
entire trip to the centre is
40Kč per adult (children
under 15 travel free). A
luggage ticket costs an
extra 20Kč.

Tickets & Passes

Tickets are interchangeable on all metros, trams and buses. Buy tickets at metro stations or nearby news stands – but never from the driver. If you're staying longer than a few hours, it's easier to buy a one-day or three-day pass. Children under 15 and seniors over 65 travel free, but have photo ID handy to show proof of age.

Short-term ticket Valid for 30 minutes; adult/concession 30/15Kč

Basic ticket Valid for 1½ hours; adult/concession 40/20Kč

One-day ticket Valid for 24 hours; adult/concession 120/60Kč

Three-day ticket Valid for 72 hours; 330Kč for all ages

Praha Hlavní Nádraží Train Station

Nearly all international trains arrive at Prague's main station, **Praha Hlavní Nádraží** (www.cd.cz), connected to the rest of the city by metro Line C.

Note that some trains arrive at Prague's other large train station, **Praha-Holešovice** (www.cd.cz), conveniently connected to the Nádraži Holešovice station by metro Line C.

Florenc Bus Station

Almost all international buses use **Florenc bus station** (www.florenc.cz), accessible by both the metro's B and C lines.

Getting Around

Prague has an excellent integrated public-transport system (www.dpp.cz) of metro lines, trams, buses and night trams, but when you're moving around the compact Old Town or the castle area, it will be more convenient – and scenic – to use your feet. Times between tram stops are posted at each stop and on the website.

Metro

○ The metro operates from 5am to midnight. Services are fast and frequent.

○ There are three lines: Line A (green) runs from Nemocnice Motol in the west to Depo Hostivař in the east; Line B (yellow) runs from Zličín in the southwest to Černý Most in the northeast; and Line C (red) runs from Háje in the southeast to Letňany in the north.

○ Handy metro stations include Staroměstská (Old Town Square), Malostranská (Malá Strana), Můstek and Muzeum (Wenceslas Square) and Hlavní Nádraží (Main Train Station).

○ You must buy a ticket (*jízdenka*) before boarding, and then validate it by punching it in the little yellow machine in the metro-station lobby or on the bus or tram when you begin your journey. Checks by inspectors are frequent.

o You'll need coins for some ticket machines at metro stations and major tram stops. You can also buy tickets at some news stands as well as tourist-information offices and metro-station ticket offices. Some machines now handle contactless cards, but your foreign bank may charge a fee for paying this way.

Tram & Bus

o Important tram lines to remember are 22/23 (runs to Prague Castle, Malá Strana and Charles Bridge), 17 and 18 (run to the Jewish Quarter and Old Town Square) and 11 (runs to Žižkov and Vinohrady).

o Regular tram and bus services operate from 5am to midnight (see www.dpp.cz for maps and timetables). After this, night trams (91 to 99) and buses (901 to 915) take over.

o All night trams intersect at Lazarská in Nové Město.

o Be aware that few tram

or bus stops sell tickets. So if you're using single tickets, buy several in the metro station or at news stands, then save a couple of unstamped ones for later and validate them upon boarding.

Taxi & Ride Share

o **Uber** (www.uber. com), **Bolt** (https://bolt. eu) and locally owned **Liftago** (www.liftago. cz) operate reliable ride-share services throughout Prague and Czechia. Download the company's app and payment information to your phone.

o Standard taxi service is widely available and generally reliable, but watch for scams. Never hail a cab directly from the street. Instead, order a taxi by phone (or ask your hotel or restaurant to do this for you). Always make sure the driver turns on the meter, and ask for a rough estimate of the fare before entering the vehicle.

o Within the city centre, shorter trips should cost from 200Kč to 300Kč. A trip to the suburbs should be no more

than 500Kč, and to the airport from 600Kč to 800Kč.

The following radio-taxi services are reliable and honest:

AAA Radio Taxi (222 333 222; www. aaataxi.cz)

City Taxi (257 257 257; www.citytaxi.cz)

Essential Information

Accessible Travel

Prague and Czechia are behind the curve when it comes to catering to travellers with disabilities. The Prague Public Transport Authority is working overtime to retrofit metro stations and tram cars to make them wheelchair-friendly, though not all stops and stations are. See www.dpp.cz for details.

o **Prague Wheelchair Users Organisation** (www.presbariery. cz) Works to promote barrier-free architecture and improve the lives of people with disabilities. Consult the website for online resources.

o **Czech Blind United**
(www.sons.cz) Represents
the vision-impaired;
provides information but
no services.

Business Hours

Banks 8am to 4.30pm
Monday to Friday

Bars 11am to midnight
or later

Main post office 2am
to midnight

Shops 8.30am to 8pm
Monday to Friday, to
6pm Saturday and
Sunday

Restaurants 10am to
11pm, though kitchens
often close by 10pm

Discount Cards

o If you intend to visit
several museums during
your stay, consider pur-
chasing a discount card
called the 'Prague Cool-
Pass' (www.praguecool
pass.com). This offers
free or discounted entry
to around 70 sights.

o Included are Prague
Castle, the Old Town
Hall, the National Gallery
museums, the Jewish
Museum, the Petřín
Lookout Tower and

Vyšehrad.

o The pass is available
for one to seven days,
starting at €76/55 per
adult/concession for
two days.

o Purchase cards online
over the website or
download the Prague
CoolPass app.

o Physical cards can also
be bought at various
museums, private tour-
ist centres and shops.

o Prague CoolPass hold-
ers are not entitled to
free travel on the city's
public-transport system.

Electricity

Type E
220V/50Hz

Type C
220V/50Hz

Emergencies

To dial a number in
Prague from outside
the country, dial your
international access
code, the Czechia
country code, then
the unique nine-digit
number.

Czechia country code	420
International access code	00
Ambulance	155
Fire	150
Police	112

Money

o Credit and debit cards
are widely accepted and
there's no need to carry
much cash around.

o The Czech crown

Money-Saving Tips

○ Forget taxis or ride shares – take public transport from the airport to the city, then walk or use the metros and trams.

○ For food, you'll find the best value meals in pubs. Plan your big meal at lunch, when many restaurants offer daily specials (look for the *'denní'* or *'polední'* menu).

○ Local beer is much cheaper than wine (and of high quality).

○ Don't exchange cash at the airport. Instead, use bank cards to pay or withdraw local currency with an ATM card.

○ Don't worry about skipping museums if cash is tight – Prague is best explored outdoors and on foot.

○ When going to the theatre, you can often get cheaper tickets for around 200Kč.

(*Koruna česká*, or Kč) is divided into 100 hellers (h), though these tiny coins no longer circulate. Prices are sometimes denominated in fractions of crowns. In these instances, the total is rounded to the nearest whole crown.

○ Keep coins handy for public toilets and tram-ticket machines.

Tipping

○ In restaurants and bars, add 10% to the tab to reward good service.

○ An easy way to figure out the tip is to round up the bill to the nearest 10Kč increment (or 50Kč or 100Kč increments on larger tabs), announce the total to the server and hand them the money.

○ Taxi drivers won't expect a tip, but it's customary to round up to the nearest 10Kč increment if they have provided special assistance.

Public Holidays

Banks, offices and some department stores and shops are closed on public holidays. Restaurants, museums and tourist attractions tend to stay open.

New Year's Day 1 January

Easter Monday March/April

Labour Day 1 May

Liberation Day 8 May

Sts Cyril & Methodius Day 5 July

Jan Hus Day 6 July

Czech Statehood Day 28 September

Republic Day 28 October

Struggle for Freedom & Democracy Day 17 November

Christmas Eve (Generous Day) 24 December

Christmas Day 25 December

St Stephen's Day 26 December

Safe Travel

Prague is a low-crime city and safer than many large cities around the world.

Dos & Don'ts

○ **Greetings** It's customary to say *dobrý den* (good day) when entering a shop, cafe or pub, and to say *na shledanou* (goodbye) when you leave. When meeting people for the first time, a firm handshake, for both men and women, is the norm.

○ **Visiting** If you're invited to someone's home, bring flowers or some other small gift for your host, and remove your shoes when you enter the house.

○ **Manners** On trams and metros, it's good manners to give up a seat to an elderly or infirm passenger.

Pickpocketing and petty theft, however, remain rife, especially around the main tourist attractions. If you are the victim of a pickpocket, report the crime as soon as possible at any nearby police station. Remember to retain any paperwork you might need for insurance purposes. For lost or stolen passports, embassies can normally issue travel documents swiftly.

Toilets

Public toilets are only free in museums, galleries, concert halls, restaurants, shopping malls and on trains. Everywhere else you have to pay – this includes in train, bus and metro stations.

Public toilets are normally staffed by attendants who charge from 10Kč upwards to use the facilities, though some automated systems have begun to make an appearance. Men's are marked *muži* or *páni,* and women's *ženy* or *dámy*.

Tourist Information

Prague City Tourism (www.prague.eu) of-fices are good sources for maps and general information, as well as an excellent resource for finding what's on. The website is in English.

The two airport branches (in the arrivals halls of both terminals) are handy for buying transport tickets as well as tickets to board the Airport Export (AE) bus from the airport to Prague's main train station. Branches also sell the discount Prague CoolPass.

Prague City Tourism – Airport (www.prague.eu)

Prague City Tourism – Rytířská (Map p90, D3; www.prague.eu)

Prague City Tourism – Old Town Hall (Map p90, C2; www.prague.eu)

Prague City Tourism – Petřín (www.prague.eu)

Visas

Generally not needed for stays of up to 90 days.

Behind the Scenes

Send Us Your Feedback

We love to hear from travellers – your comments help make our books better. We read every word, and we guarantee that your feedback goes straight to the authors. Visit **lonelyplanet.com/contact** to submit your updates and suggestions.

Note: We may edit, reproduce and incorporate your comments in Lonely Planet products such as guidebooks, websites and digital products, so let us know if you are happy to have your name acknowledged. For a copy of our privacy policy visit **lonelyplanet.com/legal**.

Marc's Thanks

Huge thanks goes to my fellow author Mark Baker for his assistance and perseverance throughout. Also a big *díky* to Paddington Tucker and Stéphane Corbet in Prague, and my wife Tanya.

Mark's Thanks

I would like to thank my friends here in Prague who always help point the way to new discoveries. I'm also grateful to my knowledgeable 'local voice': Eva Brejlová. A special thanks goes out to my editor at Lonely Planet for this project, Angela Tinson, and the book's co-author, Marc Di Duca.

Acknowledgements

Cover photograph: Old Town Square, Prague. Luciano Mortula - LGM/Shutterstock ©
Back cover photograph: Czech goulash. Stepanek Photography/ Shutterstock ©

This Book

This 7th edition of Lonely Planet's Pocket Prague was researched and written by Mark Baker and Marc Di Duca. The previous edition was also written by Mark and Marc, as well as by Barbara Woosley.

This guidebook was produced by the following:

Commissioning Editor
Angela Tinson

Product Editor
Gary Quinn

Cartographer Valentina Kremenchutskaya

Book Designer
María Virginia Moreno

Cover Researcher
Gwen Cotter

Thanks to
Imogen Bannister, Eva Brejlová, Stéphane Corbet, Shauna Daly

Index

See also separate subindexes for:

⊗ **Eating p158**

☺ **Drinking p159**

✪ **Entertainment p159**

🔒 **Shopping p159**